WOODWORKER'S POWER TOOLS:
AN ESSENTIAL GUIDE

RICK PETERS

STERLING PUBLISHING CO., INC.
New York

Production Staff

Design: Sandy Freeman
Cover Design: Karen Nelson
Photography: Christopher J. Vendetta
Cover Photo: Bill Milne

Illustrations: Triad Design Group, Ltd.
Copy Editor: Barbara McIntosh Webb
Page Layout: Sandy Freeman
Index: Nan Badgett

Every effort has been made to ensure that all the information in this book is accurate. However, due to differing conditions, tools, and individual skill, the publisher cannot be responsible for any injuries, losses, or other damages which may result from the use of information in this book.

Library of Congress Cataloging-in-Publication Data Available

10 9 8 7 6 5 4 3 2

Published by Sterling Publishing Company, Inc.
387 Park Avenue South, New York, N.Y. 10016
©2001 by Rick Peters
Distributed in Canada by Sterling Publishing
c/o Canadian Manda Group,
One Atlantic Avenue, Suite 105,
Toronto, Ontario, Canada M6K 3E7.
Distributed in Great Britain and Europe by Cassell PLC
Wellington House, 125 Strand
London WC2R 0BB, England.
Distributed in Australia by
Capricorn Link (Australia) Pty. Ltd.,
P.O. Box 704, Windsor,
NSW 2756 Australia.

Printed in China
All rights reserved

Sreling ISBN 0-8069-6659-9

CONTENTS

ACKNOWLEDGMENTS

For all their help, advice, and support, I offer special thanks to:

Christopher Vendetta, ace photographer, for taking such beautiful photographs in less than desirable conditions (my dusty workshop) and under such tight deadlines.

Bob and Mike Peters, and Mike's lovely wife, Louise, for allowing Chris and me to photograph some of their "experienced" portable power tools for the opening photos of the saws, drills, jointers and planers, and power sanders chapters.

Tony O' Malley for lending me some of his old but still quite functional power tools for the opening photos of the saws, drills, and routers chapters.

Bob Skummer and Debi Schmid of Jet Equipment & Tools for supplying photos and technical information on their most excellent Jet, Powermatic, and Performax brands.

David Sendall and Simon Kenney with Record Tools for tracking down and supplying the antique lathe photo on page 170.

Wade Walker with Porter-Cable for supplying photos, technical information, and product for the power sanders chapter.

Doug Hicks with August Home Publishing for providing the photo of the ShopNotes router table on page 137.

Doug Stephenson with Makita USA for supplying images, technical information, and product for numerous chapters.

James Taylor, Chuck Crimmel, and Carole Hollmann with Senco Products for sharing their photo of some of the first air nailers (page 146).

Jane Van Bergen with Ryobi USA for providing the image of their bench-top band saw.

Karen Powers with Freud Inc., purveyors of fine bits, blades, and power tools, for supplying images and technical information.

Sandy Freeman, book designer extraordinaire, whose exquisite art talents are evident in every page of this book.

Barb Webb, copyediting whiz, for ferreting out mistakes and gently suggesting corrections.

Greg Kopfer with the Tri-ad Design Group for his superb illustrations.

Heartfelt thanks to my family: Cheryl, Lynne, Will, and Beth, for putting up with the craziness that goes with writing a book and living with a woodworker: late nights, short weekends, wood everywhere, noise from the shop, and sawdust footprints in the house.

And finally, words can't express my gratitude to my wife Cheryl for taking off the rough edges and smoothing out the manuscript.

INTRODUCTION

My name is Rick, and I'm a power tool junkie. All kinds: portable power tools, stationary power tools—you name it, I gotta have it. There. I've said it, without benefit of a 12-step recovery program.

I've had this happy "problem" since I was 11, when my brother Jim gave me my first power tool. It was a Black & Decker finishing sander. Maybe you know the one I'm talking about: It had an ugly tan/gold plastic case with a bright orange power cord about 6 inches long (now that's useful, yes?). The sander accepted a third of a sheet of sandpaper, had one speed, and vibrated all over the place. It sounded like barbers' clippers that were out of adjustment— and I still have it. The next year, I received a B&D saber saw from my mom, and my obsession took hold.

Within a year I was doing rough and finish carpentry work with my saw and sander, and a lot of sweat and determination. My first project was a sales counter for a printing shop owned by my best friend's mom. This was my introductory "class" in the school of hard knocks. The first thing I learned? It's darned hard to make a straight cut through a 2×6 with a saber saw. So I took my first paycheck (a whopping $25) and bought a Sears circular saw. And so it went.

Like most woodworkers, my bank account balance is not as great as my zest for tools. Still, I've bought and used a lot of power tools over the years, from lightweight power screwdrivers to heavy-duty stationary equipment. I worked in over half a dozen shops and learned a lot from the seasoned old pros I worked alongside.

Now when I go to buy or use a tool, my confidence level is high. I've been there, done that. I know which tools are rugged and which aren't. And I also know that shopping for tools and using them can be simple. That's why I've written this book—to share this hard-earned information with you and boost your confidence level so that selecting and using tools is a joy, not a chore. I hope this helps.

Rick Peters
Fall 2001

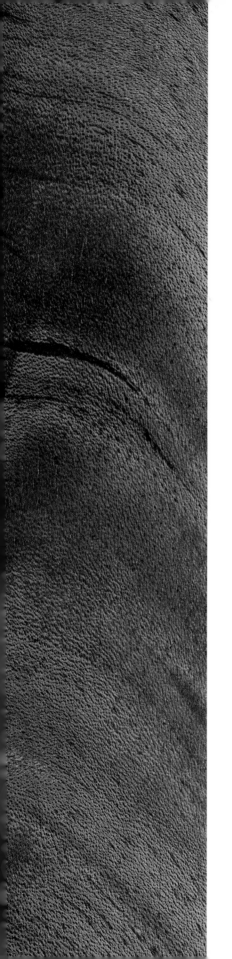

"*Of all my machines, the band saw has done the most to help me use wood the way I really want to.*"

JAMES KRENOV (1977)

POWER SAWS

The ability to "use wood the way I really want to," as Krenov puts it so succinctly, is the fundamental reason that woodworkers prize their power saws. These cutting machines are at the heart of the woodworking shop because they free the woodworker to concentrate on fine work like cutting and fitting joints instead of dimensioning lumber.

In days past, it would take a team of two men in a saw pit hours to rip a board to size. Now, thanks to power saws, it's a one-person job that takes just minutes—without raising a sweat.

Whether it's a table saw, band saw, miter saw, or circular saw (like the ones in the photo at left), power saws plow through wood fast. This is good... and bad. It's good because it makes reducing lumber to final dimensions a simple task. But it's also bad because a power saw's speed lets you make mistakes faster (sort of like a computer). And unless you have a board stretcher lying around, these mistakes can be costly.

But if treated with respect, tuned, and used properly, as Krenov observed, power saws will let you do more of what you want to in the shop.

The two rugged saws shown here are classics. *In front,* a Porter-Cable model number A-6 "Guild" saw with metal case. It features a 6-amp motor and accepts a 6" blade. *At the rear,* a Craftsman 8" electric handsaw, model number 207.25603. This hefty saw has a 10-amp motor and definitely requires two hands to operate.

TABLE SAWS

Without a doubt, the heart of any woodworking shop is the table saw. This hardworking tool is used for ripping, cross-cutting, miters, bevels, joinery—even shaping edges. There is a huge array of accessories available for the table saw—everything from box-joint jigs to sanding disks. There are three main models of table saw to choose from: bench-tops saws, contractor's saws, and cabinet saws.

Bench-top saw

A bench-top saw like the one shown in the top photo is a good choice for a woodworker with limited space. These saws typically have smaller motors and are direct-drive. Because of this, they're good for light jobs but should not be used for heavy work such as ripping thick stock. If you do need to do this with this type of saw, slow down your feed rate to keep the small motor from bogging down. Woodworkers who work primarily on smaller projects (like birdhouses, or model making) find these quite sufficient.

Contractor's saw

The next step up in table saws is the "contractor's" saw like the one shown in the bottom photo. These saws are rugged, portable, and hardworking and have become extremely popular with contractors (hence the name). A contractor's saw is identifiable by its rear-mounted motor. Mounting the motor like this makes it easy for a framer or trim carpenter to set the saw on a pair of sawhorses and go right to work. For years all I ever used was a contractor's saw, and this is an excellent choice for most woodworkers. Many saw manufacturers now offer these saws with large tables and super-accurate fences. A well-tuned contractor's saw can rival the performance of a cabinet saw (*see the opposite page*)—and they cost hundreds less.

Photo courtesy of Makita USA, copyright 2001

Photo courtesy of Jet Equipment & Tools, copyright 2001

Cabinet saw

When most woodworkers dream of the ultimate saw, they have a cabinet saw in mind (often called a tilting-arbor saw) like the one shown in the top photo. A cabinet saw features a closed-in base, a large motor (often 3-hp), and heavy-duty castings. These cost in the $1,200 to $1,500 range and are hard to justify for the occasional woodworker. If you do a lot of woodworking (or can just plain afford it), I'd recommend buying a cabinet saw. A quality saw is vibration-free and cuts through even the thickest stock with ease. They're generally more accurate than the other types and will last a lifetime if maintained properly.

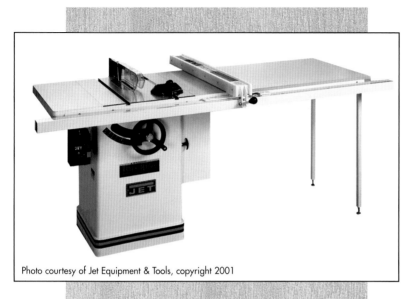

Photo courtesy of Jet Equipment & Tools, copyright 2001

Anatomy

Bench-top, contractor's, and cabinet saws all basically have the same parts—what's different is the size and quality (*bottom drawing*). At its simplest, a table saw consists of a blade attached to the shaft of a motor. The blade protrudes through a slot in the table and is raised or lowered as needed. It can also be tilted from side to side for bevel cuts. The blade should be protected by some type of guard—typically high-impact clear plastic.

For rip cuts, a fence attaches to the table so it's parallel to the blade. This fence rides on round or square bars or extrusions that attach to the table's front and back top edge. For cross cuts, slots in the table accept a miter gauge (and other accessories, such as a tenoning jig).

Bench-top and contractor's saws attach to a steel base to bring the table up to a comfortable working height. Cabinet saws usually have a closed-in base that houses a motor that connects to the saw arbor via V-belts. Closing in the base like this reduces noise and also allows for efficient dust collection.

On contractor's saws, the motor is usually mounted on the back of the table saw and again is connected to the saw arbor via a belt. Bench-top saws typically have the blade attached directly to the motor shaft.

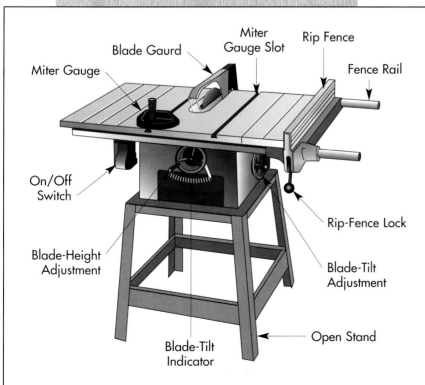

TABLE SAW FEATURES

Table

Often overlooked, the quality, type, and size of the table of a table saw is an important feature worth looking into. Since most table tops on most saws are cast iron, it's important that it be true and flat. To further extend the working surface of the top, most have an extension wing attached to each side. These may be stamped metal (*as shown in the top photo*), or cast iron. If you're looking for added rigidity, with the added benefit of dampened vibrations, consider paying the extra for cast-iron wings. The slots in the table top are also important. T-shaped slots (like those shown here) capture the miter gauge over much of its travel, preventing it from tipping up and causing a nasty accident.

Blade diameter

The maximum-diameter blade that the saw can accept will greatly affect its maximum depth (*middle photo*). Most contractor's and cabinet saws take a 10" blade and can cut through stock that's over 3" thick. Smaller bench-top saws often take an 8" blade (or smaller) and can only handle stock around 2" in thickness. Note that most dado blades are 8" or less in diameter. That's because when fitted with all chippers, they can remove a lot of wood. The manufacturers decrease the diameter so that you can't damage your saw by trying to take too hefty a cut (the smaller diameters are also safer).

Motor size

Motor size will also play a large role in your saw's performance—particularly when cutting thin stock or dense woods. A small motor will bog down and sometimes even stall. Most contractor's saws have a 1$\frac{1}{2}$-hp motor—big enough for most woodworkers (*bottom photo*). If on the other hand you tend to work with thick stock and/or work a saw hard, you're better off getting a saw with a

larger motor. Most cabinet saws use a 3-hp motor, which is powerful enough to plow through almost anything in a single pass. An item to note: 3-hp saws typically require 220 volts to operate—if your shop only has 110 volts, stick with a contractor's saw—they require only 110 volts (but it's smart to have it on its own 20-amp breaker).

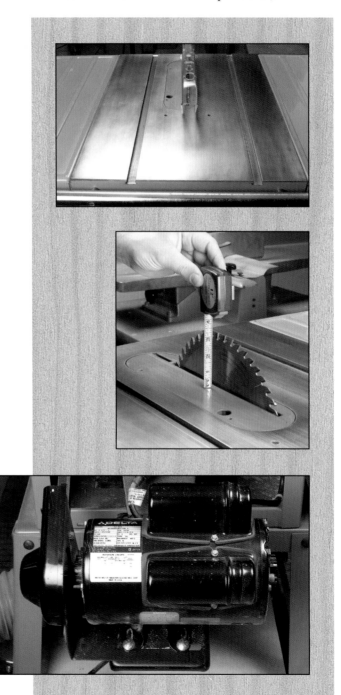

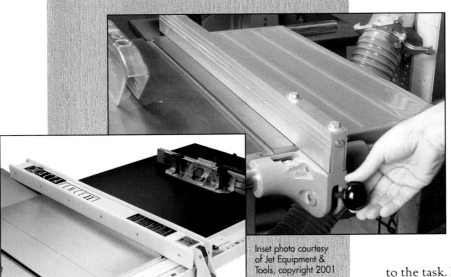

Inset photo courtesy
of Jet Equipment &
Tools, copyright 2001

Rip fences

If you're going to spend money on a single table saw upgrade, consider replacing the standard rip fence (*top photo*). An accurate rip fence, like the one shown in the inset photo, can make all the difference between an average project and an extraordinary project. Since the table saw is used along with the jointer and planer to produce square stock to begin with (*see pages 96–97 for more on this*), it's imperative that your rip fence be equal to the task. If you're off by even half a degree, your joints won't fit, boards won't glue up properly, and your projects will suffer.

Miter gauges

The miter gauge that comes with most table saws is adequate for rough work (*middle photo*). As long as you fine-tune the stops, it'll do for most close-tolerance work as well. Just make sure there's no slop in the miter gauge bar—that is, you can't wiggle it from side to side. If there is movement, either apply a strip of metal tape (the kind used to seal stove pipe) or create a couple dimples on the side of the bar by tapping it with a centerpunch and a hammer. For the ultimate in accuracy, there are a number of high-quality after-market miter gauges available.

TABLE SAW RECOMMENDATIONS

If money is no object, by all means purchase a cabinet saw. Your only tough decision here will be to get a tilt-left or a tilt-right. I prefer a tilt-left, as the blade pivots away from the rip fence for bevel cuts. If you're on a budget (like most of us), a contractor's saw is a good choice. I would, however, recommend that you invest in a quality after-market rip fence because this can make a huge difference in accuracy. Finally, if space is a concern, consider a smaller bench-top version—or if you need more power, buy a contractor's saw and spring for a mobile base.

TABLE SAW ACCESSORIES

Saw blades

There are two types of saw blades out there: high-speed steel (HSS) and carbide-tipped. As far as I'm concerned the majority of the HSS blades out there are best used for shop clocks. Carbide-tipped is the only way to go (*top photo*). The only advantage HSS blades offer (besides being cheaper) is that they're less expensive to sharpen. But this is offset by the frequent number of sharpenings the blade will need. That's carbide's big claim to fame—a carbide-tipped blade will stay sharper a whole lot longer than HSS—and it can be resharpened as well (just make sure you use a sharpening service that's experienced with carbide). The quality of the blade will have much to do with the thickness and quality of the carbide, so go with a name you can trust (I'm a Freud man, myself).

Profiles

Table saw blades are available in numerous profiles and configurations. You can get blades designed just for ripping (few teeth, flat-top grind) or cross-cutting (many teeth, ATB grind), or the most common, a combination blade (typically, ATB with a raker tooth); *see the middle drawing.* Triple-chip and flat grind is another popular choice for combination blades. Note that the slots cut into some of the blades in the middle drawing are designed to help reduce vibration. For general-purpose work, a combination blade is your best bet—I prefer a 40-tooth ATB and raker blade. But I also have a 16-tooth rip blade that's worth putting on when I need to rip a lot of stock.

Dado sets

In addition to a good-quality combination blade, you'll want to get a dado set (*bottom photo*).

Photo courtesy of Freud Inc., copyright 2001

FLAT-TOP GRIND

TRIPLE-CHIP AND FLAT GRIND

ATB AND RAKER

ATB (ATLERNATE-TOP BEVEL)

Photo courtesy of Freud Inc., copyright 2001

Dado sets are basically two blades with chippers sandwiched in between. Varying the number of chippers changes the width of the dado. Fine adjustments can be made by adding or removing shims between chippers. I use my dado set a lot and have a healthy respect for it. Of all the blades, this one has the greatest ability to chew up your hands. That's why I recommend buying a "safety" dado set. Freud makes a set that has

Photo courtesy of
Freud Inc., copyright 2001

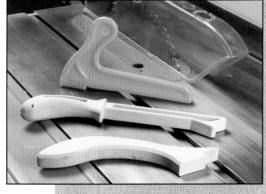

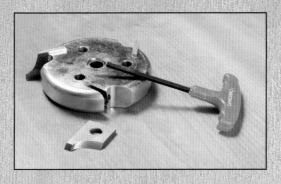

kickback-reducing limitators on both the outer blades and the chippers, which greatly reduce the danger of kickback from overfeeding.

Blade stabilizers

If you've never used a set of blade stabilizers, I recommend giving them a try. Blade stabilizers are a set of precision-machined and balanced plates that fit on both sides of the blade (*top photo*). They not only improve the cut by reducing blade vibration, but they also help the saw to run quieter. Reducing vibration also helps extend saw life. Most stabilizers are designed for blades 7" in diameter and larger and are intended only for use with stationary saws.

Push sticks

Push sticks are finger savers—need I say more? Whether you make you own or purchase them, push sticks are designed to push a workpiece safely past a spinning blade (*middle photo*). Of course for these to do any good, they have to be used. I got nicked just once when I started woodworking and have been an evangelist for push sticks ever since. Keep several on hand, and use them whenever a cut would bring your hand close enough to contact the blade.

Molding heads

Although I have some woodworking buddies who swear by them, I'll admit I've had mixed results with molding heads like the one shown in the bottom photo. Molding heads accept a wide variety of cutters and can virtually turn your table saw into a router or shaper. The problem is that I've never been comfortable with those knives spinning near my hands. I much prefer a table-mounted router—they're easier to set up and to use (*see page* 137 *for more on this*). On the other hand, the power that a table saw offers allows you to cut a joint in a single pass (I guess that's what makes me nervous). Since I'm never in that much of a hurry, I'll stick with my router.

TABLE SAW ALIGNMENT

Since you depend on the table saw for accurate cuts, it's important to know how to fine-tune it so it can provide the precision you desire. What many woodworkers fail to realize is that a brand new table is often in need of this fine-tuning. Unfortunately, most manuals don't mention this, and the resulting frustration can lead to diminished enthusiasm for the craft. That's too bad, because tuning or aligning a table saw isn't that difficult—it just takes a little know-how and some patience.

The trunion

In order for a table saw to cut accurately, the blade must be parallel to the rip fence and perpendicular to the miter gauge. The carriage that holds the blade and allows it to be raised up and down and tilted for bevel cuts is called the trunion. The trunion typically attaches to the table top by way of four bolts (*bottom drawing*). To adjust the orientation of the blade, you'll need to locate and adjust these four bolts; *see below*.

Checking the alignment

To check the trunion's alignment, start by unplugging the saw. Then install a blade and mark one of the teeth with a marker. Next, press the body of a combination square firmly against the right edge of the miter gauge slot and extend the blade out until it just touches the marked tooth, as shown in the top photo. Then rotate the blade counterclockwise and slide the combination square in the miter gauge slot until it aligns with the marked tooth (*middle photo*). If the trunion is in alignment, the blade will just barely touch the tooth as it did in the forward position. If it doesn't, loosen the trunion bolts to friction-tight and tap the trunion casting with a rubber mallet to bring it into alignment. Repeat the check and tighten the bolts when it's in alignment.

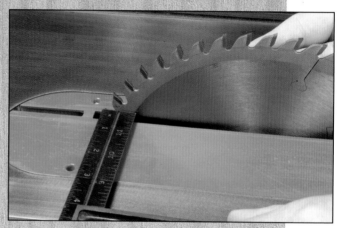

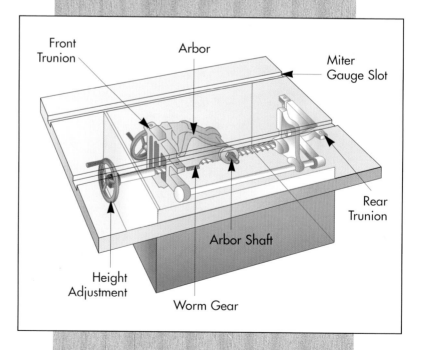

Front Trunion

Arbor

Miter Gauge Slot

Rear Trunion

Arbor Shaft

Worm Gear

Height Adjustment

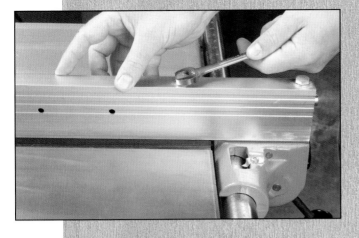

A perfectly aligned trunion is the starting point for accurate cuts. Once it's aligned, you can fine-tune the other parts. Note: Don't skip this important step—if you align other parts to a misaligned trunion, only headaches will result.

Rip fence

Since you used the miter gauge slots as the reference to align the trunion, you can use these to align the rip fence. Simply slide your fence over until one edge is flush with the edge of the miter gauge slot. Then loosen the rip fence mounting bolts to friction-tight, and tap the top of the fence until it aligns with the edge of the miter gauge slot (*top photo*). Retighten the bolts to lock the aligned fence in place. Note that some woodworkers prefer to pivot the top end of the fence a tiny bit off parallel to help prevent binding. I don't recommend this, since it's not necessary if your trunion is aligned.

Miter gauge

The are a number of ways to make sure your miter gauge is perpendicular to the saw blade. I've always found a try square works well. Just press the long blade against the body of the miter gauge, and slide it over until the short blade butts up against the saw blade (*middle photo*). Make sure to rotate the blade so the try square presses against the blade and not the carbide tips. Then loosen the miter gauge handle and adjust the position of the head until the short leg of the try square butts squarely up against the saw blade. Tighten the miter gauge handle and adjust the 90-degree stop (usually a setscrew).

Blade perpendicular to table

Finally, it's important to make sure the saw blade is perpendicular to the table. Raise the blade as high as it will go, and place a try square up against the blade (*bottom photo*). Tilt the blade as necessary to align it, then adjust the 90-degree stop (see your owner's manual). Then tilt the blade to 45 degrees and check this as well (*inset photo*). Adjust the tilt as necessary, and fine-tune the stop if required.

TABLE SAW SAFETY

Before delving into the basic cuts on the table saw, I'd like to spend some time covering safety on the table saw. Even the motor on a small bench-top table saw has sufficient torque to power a saw blade through your hand. And on the larger saws, this can happen in the blink of an eye. I'd say at least half of the woodworkers I've had the pleasure of meeting over the years (and there are thousands) have had a run-in with a table saw. Some just got nicked, while others are missing parts of fingers. I'm not trying to scare you, but I would like to imbue in you a healthy respect for this powerful but dangerous machine. With good safety habits, you can greatly reduce the chances of an accident.

Basic safety

There are a few hard and fast safety rules for the table saw. Number 1: Always use the blade guard (note that the guard is removed for clarity in many of the photos of this book—but you can tell I'm a religious user of this important safety device by looking at my hands—all fingers intact!). Number 2: Use a push stick whenever possible (*top photo*). These really are finger savers. Number 3: Listen to that little voice in your head when it tells you that the cut you're about to make looks dangerous. There's most likely a safer way—stop and figure it out.

Pinch cuts

In addition to the basic safety rules described above, the other common causes of accidents with the table saw are created by pinch points—that is, a workpiece gets pinched between the spinning blade and the rip fence. The result is a dangerous event called kickback. Basically, the saw blade grabs the workpiece and hurtles it back toward you with incredible force, often pulling your fingers (if you're not using a push stick) into the blade. You can help avoid this by making sure your rip fence is aligned properly and doesn't toe in toward the

blade (*middle photo*). Also, never make a through cut with the miter gauge using the rip fence as a stop (*bottom photo*)—this is an accident waiting to happen.

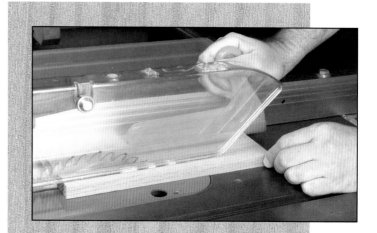

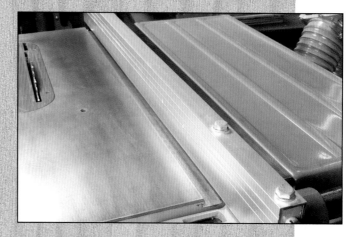

TABLE SAW: RIPPING

Ripping is one of the most basic tasks for the table saw. A properly adjusted trunion and rip

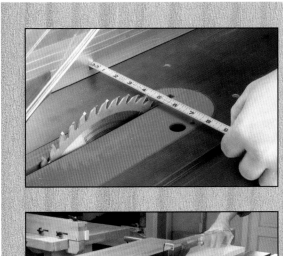

fence will make this a simple task. As a general rule of thumb, you should raise the blade so that it's about $1/4$" higher than the thickness of the workpiece. Saw manufacturers often suggest having at least three teeth in the stock at all times, and on most blades this is what you'll have if you use the $1/4$" rule.

Fence position

To rip a board to width, start by positioning the rip fence for the desired cut. Unless you have an after-market rip fence that's known for accuracy, I don't recommend using the graduations that are stamped or etched into the rip fence rails for positioning. Even if you align the indicator, variations in the markings can lead to inaccuracy. I prefer to measure from the rip fence to the blade teeth with a tape measure (*top photo*). Here again, if everything is aligned, you'll need to measure only in one place.

Use support

In many instances the stock you're ripping will be long. In cases like this, it's important to fully support the stock after it's cut. If you don't, the weight of the unsupported end can cause the other end to tilt up—a dangerous situation. The simplest way to prevent this is to use an outfeed roller support, like the one shown in the middle photo.

ZERO-CLEARANCE INSERT

A zero-clearance insert is a special shop-made insert that hugs the blade and prevents thin strips from dropping down into the normal wider blade slot. A built-in splitter also helps prevent binding (*bottom drawing*).

You can use your standard insert as a template to make a zero-clearance insert. First, place the standard insert on a $1/2$"-thick piece of plywood and trace around it. Then cut it to rough shape to within $1/8$" of the outline. Next, temporarily attach the standard insert to the plywood with double-sided tape. Now you can trim it to exact size with a flush-trim bit in a router. Drill a 1" lift-out hole in the insert, and cut a kerf in it for a splitter that aligns with the blade. Glue a $1/8$" piece of hardboard in the end of the kerf, and you're ready to rip safely.

Splitter

$3/4$" Finger Hole

$1/2$"-Thick Plywood

TABLE SAW: CROSS CUTS

The other most basic task you'll use the table saw for is cross-cutting. Now I'll be honest and tell you that I use my table saw only for finish cross cuts and for joinery. I use my sliding compound miter saw (*see page* 30) for rough cross-cutting, especially long boards. That's because it's awkward at best to cross-cut a long board on the table saw. If this is your only saw, though, there are a couple things you can do to make this less awkward; *see below.*

Miter gauge

The same $1/4$" rule that I discussed for ripping applies with cross cuts: About $1/4$" of the blade should extend up past the top of the workpiece during the cut. Place the workpiece on the miter gauge, and slide it over until the marked cut line aligns with the left edge of the saw teeth (*top photo*). Turn on the saw, make a tentative kerf in the edge, and pull the miter gauge to see whether it's cutting where you marked. Adjust as necessary, and push the workpiece through the blade to finish the cut.

Auxiliary fence

One way to help stabilize a long board is to attach a wood auxiliary fence to the body of the miter gauge. There are holes in the body just for this purpose. If you extend the fence an inch or two past the saw blade, it will also support the cutoff and prevent tear-out (*middle photo*). For super-accurate cross cuts, I like to clamp a stop to the auxiliary fence (*bottom photo*). This also makes it easy to duplicate parts. ShopTip: To prevent the workpiece from "creeping" or shifting during the cut, apply a piece of sandpaper to the face of the auxiliary fence. The grit of the paper will help grip the workpiece.

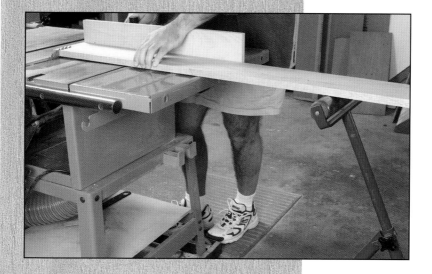

Support

Even when you attach an auxiliary fence to the miter gauge body, it can still be a challenge to safely cross-cut a long board on the table saw. That's because the unsupported end can tip down and raise the end near the blade—again a dangerous situation. To prevent this from happening, consider using some type of side support. An outfeed roller can help. Just be sure to orient the roller parallel to the table (*top photo*). Another method is to position your saw near a table or workbench that's of similar height and use this to support the board. (I have a friend who blocked up his workbench so that it's about ¹⁄₂" lower than the table of the saw—he says it works great.)

Panels

Cross-cutting sheet stock can also be a challenge on the table saw, particularly when the needed cut exceeds the maximum cut allowed by the rip fence (24" in most stand-alone contractor's saws). Here are a couple tricks for handling this potentially dangerous cut. First, you can clamp an "outrigger" to the underside of the panel you're cutting to serve as a surrogate rip fence. Position a known-straight scrap of wood that's about twice as long as your saw's table so that the marked cut line on the plywood aligns with the blade. When it's in position, clamp it firmly in place and make the cut by pressing the outrigger firmly against the left edge of the table, as shown in the middle photo.

Another option that's useful for pieces that are too wide for the miter gauge (that is, the body extends past the front edge of the saw if you pull it out far enough to make the cut) is to reverse the miter gauge (*bottom photo*). This technique requires a steady hand, and you must make sure to press the workpiece firmly into the body of the miter gauge throughout the cut.

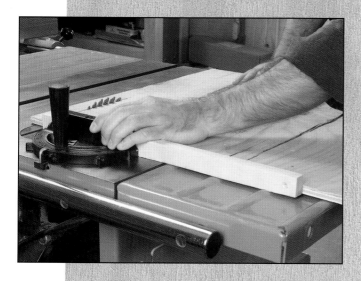

TABLE SAW: STACKED-DADO SET

In addition to ripping and cross-cutting, the other task that I most often use the table saw for is joinery. It excels at cutting grooves, dadoes, and rabbets. And for the majority of these, I use a stacked-dado set.

Install stack

A stacked-dado set consists of two outer blades and a set of chippers that are sandwiched between the blades. Varying the number of chippers determines the width of the cut (*top drawing*). For the best balance (and minimal vibration), it's important to install the chippers so they're spread out evenly along the perimeter of the blade. For two chippers, install them perpendicular to each other; for three, space them out like those shown in the top drawing. Note: You can fine-tune the width by inserting round shims between the chippers—the plastic lids from coffee cans work great.

Also, make sure to tighten the arbor nut securely and then install a molding head insert (*middle photo*). This type of insert has a wide notch to allow the dado stack to pass through safely. An even safer version is to make your own zero-clearance insert (*see page 17*). Just trim the splitter so it's flush with the top of the insert (otherwise it can interfere with the cut).

Test cut

I'm a test cut kind of guy. I believe in the "sneak-up-on-it" approach to fitting joints. I always make a test cut in scrap before making the cuts on my project pieces. A test cut will ensure that the dado set is the correct width and the correct height and that the dado is the correct distance from the edge. If possible, I like to test the fit by trying to slip the mating part in the dado, groove, or rabbet I just cut (*bottom photo*). Accurate measuring is wonderful, but there's no substitute for a nice "squeaky" fit.

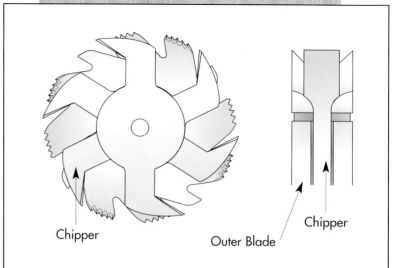

Chipper

Outer Blade

Chipper

Rabbets

Cutting a rabbet along the edge of a board with a stacked-dado set requires some additional preparation to make the cut safely. That's because the dado stack needs to be flush with the rip fence. Since this would inevitably cause damage to the rip fence, the solution is to attach a wood auxiliary fence to the rip fence and "bury" the stacked-dado set in the wood fence. To do this, attach a wood fence to the rip fence with screws. Then lower the dado set and position the wood fence over the set so the desired amount is exposed. Next, turn on the saw and raise the dado set to the desired height. Make a test cut, and adjust as necessary (*top photo*). Here again, you'll be better off starting low and sneaking up on the final height.

Grooves

Stacked-dado sets are my favorite way to cut grooves in a workpiece. That's because I can make the cut in a single pass (*middle photo*). A quality dado set will leave a flat-bottom groove that rivals that made by a straight bit in a router. Note that if you do notice a "stepped" bottom, it may be possible to eliminate this by replacing the offending chipper (usually the one that is protruding too far). A quality saw-sharpening service can also true your chippers up for you—it's well worth the cost. SAFETY NOTE: Don't be lured into a false sense of security while making dado cuts because the blade is buried in the stock—you should still use a push stick to feed the stock into the blade—never press your hand on the workpiece as it passes over the dado set.

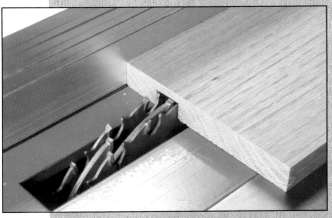

Dadoes

I also use a dado set for cutting grooves (*bottom photo*). First of all, it's best to attach an auxiliary fence to the miter gauge so it extends out past the dado set for these cuts. The fence will back up the cut and prevent splintering as it exits the workpiece. Also, as long as your trunion, rip fence, and miter gauge are aligned, it's safe to use the rip fence as a stop to define the cut. What makes it safe here is that it's not a through cut—there's no cutoff to be pinched between the rip fence and the blade.

Band Saws

As Krenov mentioned in the beginning of this chapter, the band saw has helped him to do what he wanted with wood more than any other tool. Many woodworkers feel that strongly about the band saw. In fact, some suggest that it be your first stationary tool purchase. Although I still feel the table saw is the best first stationary tool, the band saw is right up there. This may surprise some, because many feel the band saw is just a curve-cutting machine. It is that—and more. I use my band saw often for joinery. I cut tenons on it regularly, and even define the tails and pins of dovetails. I also use it frequently to resaw stock and occasionally to make my own veneer. It really is a versatile machine. There are two main types of band saw available: bench-top and stationary.

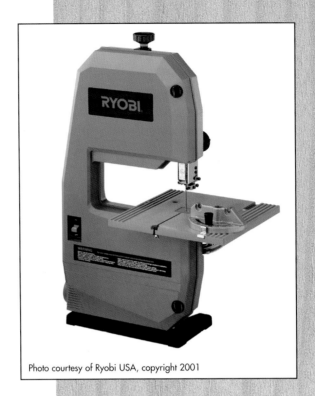

Photo courtesy of Ryobi USA, copyright 2001

Bench-top band saws

Bench-top band saws are a good choice for woodworkers with limited shop space (*top photo*). Their diminutive size and light weight make it easy to store them out of the way when not in use. They're designed to rest on a workbench and often employ direct-drive motors— that is, the motor shaft turns the drive wheel of the saw directly. Bench-top band saws typically have smaller throat and maximum-cut capacities than stationary band saws. These saws can handle most tasks but should be used sparingly for heavy resawing since they're just not built for this type of work.

Stationary band saws

A stationary band saw is a larger version of the bench-top saw that's built with heavy castings and larger capacities (*bottom photo*). The size that's most often found in the woodworking shop is a 14" saw that can handle stock up to 6" in thickness. Stationary band saws are available with either an open or closed stand. A closed stand makes it easier to collect and convey dust and chips to a collector.

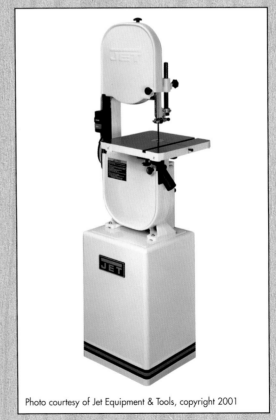

Photo courtesy of Jet Equipment & Tools, copyright 2001

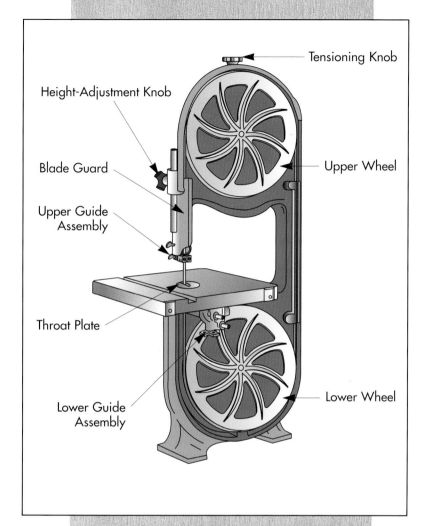

Tensioning Knob

Height-Adjustment Knob

Blade Guard

Upper Guide
Assembly

Throat Plate

Lower Guide
Assembly

Upper Wheel

Lower Wheel

The blade of a band saw is a continuous toothed band that rides on a pair of wheels (*top drawing*). Both wheels are lined with rubber to grip the blade and hold it in position. The bottom wheel is the drive wheel and is either connected directly to the motor or is turned via pulleys and a V-belt. The top wheel tilts forward and backward to "track" the blade on the wheels. Commonly, the tracking adjustment is a pair of locking knobs on the back of the saw case near the top wheel. The top wheel is also connected to a mechanism that raises and lowers the wheel by way of a knob on top to increase or decrease the tension on the blade.

The blade is supported near the workpiece by way of two guide assemblies: an upper and a lower. Each of these guide assemblies contains a thrust bearing and a pair of guide blocks (or bearings) that help keep the blade in place and support it during a cut. The lower guide assembly is fixed in place, and the upper guide assembly, along with the blade guard, can be raised up or down as needed. The table of the saw can be tilted for bevel cuts and has a slot for a miter gauge. A kerf in the table allows you to remove and replace blades (*for more on this, see page 26*).

BAND SAW RECOMMENDATIONS

If space allows and you can afford it, I'd recommend buying a stationary band saw—preferably a 14" model with a closed stand. This saw will last a lifetime and will stand up to heavy use. I've been using my band saw hard for the last 20 years and have only had to replace the thrust bearings and guide blocks twice. Go with a name you can trust; both Jet and Delta make quality stationary band saws. Look for one with smooth castings, a powerful motor, and an easy-to-change blade. Make sure that replacement parts will be available in the future. (It's a good idea to actually order a couple of spare thrust bearings and guide blocks when you purchase your saw—they'll eventually fail, and you'll be glad you have them on hand.)

BAND SAW FEATURES

There are a number of features to examine when you're looking to purchase a band saw: capacity, table tilt, and the fence system.

Capacity

There are two basic capacities with which you should concern yourself with a band saw: throat size and maximum depth of cut. The throat size is the distance from the blade to the casing of the saw (*top drawing*). This defines the widest piece you can cut. Some manufacturers double this. For example, if the throat capacity is 12", they'll say you can cut to the center of a 24"-wide panel. The maximum depth of cut is the distance from the table to the bottom of the upper guide assembly and defines the maximum thickness of stock you can cut. Although I find 6" to be sufficient, some manufacturers sell an optional spacer that extends the upper wheel up to increase the maximum depth of cut.

Table

The table of the band saw is also worth taking a close look at. First of all, the casting should be flat and smooth, and the miter gauge slot should be well-machined. The table should also tilt for bevel cuts (*middle photo*). Take the time to tilt it to see how easy this is to do, paying particular attention to the locking knob and indicator. Note: The indicator should be used only for rough positioning; use a bevel gauge and/or a protractor to make the final adjustment.

Fence

In my opinion, a rip fence is an essential accessory for the band saw (*bottom photo*). You can purchase a manufacturer's rip fence, buy an after-market fence, or make your own (ShopNotes magazine Issue #8 at www.backissuesstore.com offers plans for a nifty shop-made band saw fence system). Look for a fence that offers built-in stops and can be adjusted to compensate for blade drift (more on this later).

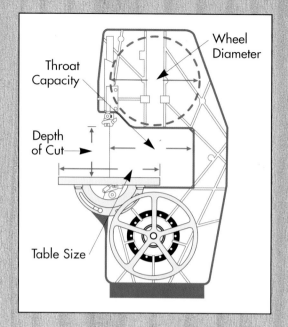

Throat Capacity

Wheel Diameter

Depth of Cut

Table Size

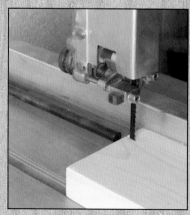

BAND SAW BLADES

Band saw blades are available in a few different types and blade profiles. They come in a wide variety of lengths and can also be custom-ordered to fit just about any saw. The standard length for a 14" band saw is $93\frac{1}{2}$".

Types of blades

Band saw blades come in three basic types: carbon steel, bi-metal, and carbide-tipped. Both the carbon steel and bi-metal blades work well, although the bi-metal blades tend to stay sharper a bit longer (*top photo*). Blade widths for the average band saw vary from a delicate $\frac{1}{8}$" (these usually require a special set of guide blocks) up to 1". The wider blades are most often used for resawing, and this is the style that you're most likely to see carbide-tipped. A wide blade helps when resawing but can't handle curves well. The narrower the blade, the tighter a radius you can turn (*middle drawing*). I keep a stock of $\frac{1}{4}$"- and $\frac{3}{4}$"-wide blades on hand. I leave the $\frac{1}{4}$" blade in the saw unless I'm resawing, then I switch to the $\frac{3}{4}$"-wide blade.

Profiles

In addition to its length and width, there are a couple of other things you'll need to specify when ordering a band saw blade. You'll also need to pick a tooth profile and the type of set. Common profiles are hook-tooth, skip-tooth, and standard (*bottom drawing*). I recommend a skip-tooth blade with a raker set. This style blade will handle most cutting jobs in the shop. For resawing, I recommend a hook-tooth blade because it does a better job of clearing the kerf of sawdust (and there's a whole lot of that when resawing). Keeping the kerf clear will keep the blade cooler and running straighter.

$\frac{1}{4}$" Blade
$\frac{3}{4}$" Radius

$\frac{1}{2}$" Blade
$1\frac{1}{4}$" Radius

$\frac{3}{16}$" Blade
$\frac{1}{2}$" Radius

$\frac{1}{8}$" Blade
$\frac{1}{4}$" Radius

$\frac{3}{4}$" Blade
$2\frac{1}{2}$" Radius

HOOK-TOOTH BLADE

SKIP-TOOTH BLADE

STANDARD BLADE

BAND SAW TUNE-UP

A properly tuned band saw is a joy to use. One that's out of alignment will "throw" blades, produce inaccurate cuts, and generally struggle through a sawing task. Fortunately, tuning a band saw is a simple task—and something that you'll need to do every time you change a blade.

Removing and installing blades

To install a new blade and tune your saw, unplug the saw and loosen the blade tension. Then if necessary, remove the front fence rail and/or the pin that aligns the table halves where the kerf is cut for blade access. Next, I advise backing off the thrust bearings and guide blocks to make it easy to remove and install the blade (*see the opposite page*). Now lift out the throat plate and remove the blade from the saw (*top photo*).

Adjusting tension

With the new blade centered on the upper and lower wheels, gradually increase the tension by turning the tension adjustment (*middle photo*). Most manufacturers have a tension indicator inside the saw's case. This indicator is calibrated to match the width of the blade. After it's tensioned, give the top wheel a spin (I recommend using a short length of dowel for this, to keep from pinching your fingers) to see whether the blade is tracking—that is, remaining centered on the wheels. If it isn't, loosen the tracking lock knob and adjust the tracking knob until the blade tracks evenly (see your owner's manual).

Guide assembly anatomy

The guide assembly supports the blade directly above and below the cut. Once the blade is tracking, you can adjust the thrust bearings and guide blocks, which help hold the blade in position (*see the opposite page*). Each guide assembly has a pair of guide blocks that can be adjusted side to side independently and back and forth as a unit (*bottom drawing*). Each thrust bearing is also adjustable in and out.

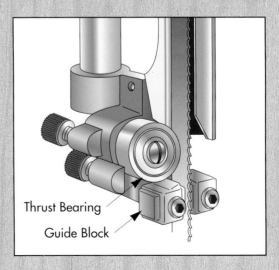

Thrust Bearing

Guide Block

Adjusting thrust bearings

The purpose of the thrust bearing is to prevent the workpiece from forcing the blade off the wheels during a cut. Basically, the blade butts up against it and can't go back any further. Because it's a bearing, it spins as the blade rubs up against it—and this keeps the blade from scoring the bearing. To prevent excess wear of the bearing, it should be adjusted so it contacts the blade only when stock is being cut. If you slip a folded dollar bill between the blade and the bearing and adjust for a snug fit, you'll have the correct clearance (*top photo*).

Adjusting guide blocks

How you adjust the guide blocks will depend on what type they are. The are three common types: metal, composite, and bearing systems. Since I recommend the composite type, I'll cover how to adjust them. Here again, a dollar bill works as a nifty feeler gauge: Just wrap it around the blade, and press the guide blocks in for a snug fit (*middle photo*). Tighten the setscrews and run the machine to see that it runs smoothly. Metal blocks generally need a bit more clearance because both the blade and the blocks will wear if they come in contact with each other; consult your owner's manual for proper clearance.

Once the guide blocks are adjusted from side to side, you can adjust them from front to back. Typically, there's a double locking knob setup that adjusts the lower assembly in and out. Loosen the lock knob and turn the adjustment knob until the guide blocks support the blade without coming in contact with the teeth (*bottom drawing*). Then twist the locking knob to secure the assembly.

Thrust Bearing Setscrew

Guide Block Adjustment

Guide Block Thumbscrew

Position Guide Block Just behind Teeth

BAND SAW CUTS

Like a table saw, a band saw is a powerful yet dangerous machine. Band saws, after all, are what butchers use to slice meat. The spinning blade of a band saw will cut through a finger as easily as through a piece of wood. Here again, I'm not trying to frighten you, just instill a healthy respect for the tool. As always, safe operating principles will prevent the majority of accidents. And just as with a table saw, use the guard, and use a push stick whenever your hand gets near the blade.

Straight cuts

Although the band saw is known as a curve-cutting machine, I make a surprising number of straight cuts with it. Since I usually joint the edges of a board that I rip to width, I find myself using a band saw often to rip pieces to width—particularly short stock that would be unsafe to cut on the table saw. Just position the rip fence for the desired width and lock it in place. Lower the blade guard so it's as close as it can be to the workpiece without actually touching it. Note that if you're freehand-cutting a workpiece (that is, you're not using the fence), you may want to raise the guard about 1/4" above the workpiece—this makes it easier to see the cut line. Turn on the saw and push the workpiece into the cut (*top photo*). As you near the end, switch to a push stick to guide it safely past the blade.

Curved cuts

Curved cuts are easy on the band saw; just make sure that you know the radius limitations of the blade (*see page 25*). Gentle curves are a snap to cut, as it's just a matter of following your cut line (*middle photo*). For circle cuts, try pressing down near the center of the workpiece and rotating the workpiece into the blade—you can get a surprisingly accurate circle this way. For tight curves, you may find it necessary to cut a series of relief slots in the workpiece to free up cutoffs through the curve (*bottom photo*). This technique can be used for all cuts to help reduce the weight of the workpiece by removing the waste.

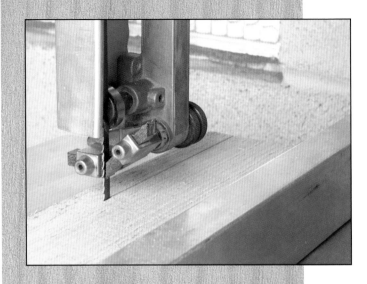

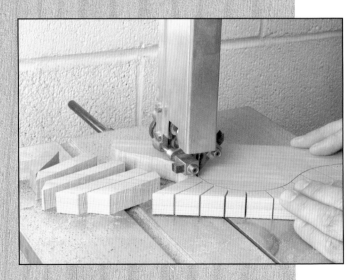

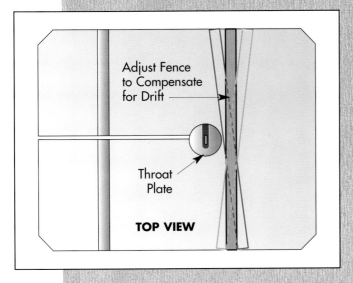

Adjust Fence to Compensate for Drift

Throat Plate

TOP VIEW

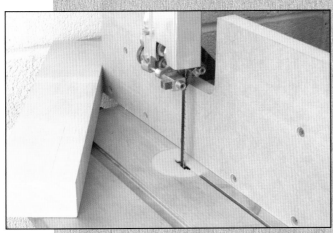

RESAWING

Resawing is a technique where you cut through the width of a workpiece to create thinner stock. A common problem that occurs when resawing is "drift." Drift is a blade's tendency to pull a workpiece in one direction. It's caused by a blade that has been improperly set—that is, the set (the amount each tooth is bent away from the blade) is not the same on both sides. To compensate for drift, you'll need to shift the fence from parallel (*top drawing*). To see if your blade drifts, make a cut in a scrap and let the blade guide the wood. If it drifts, leave the scrap in place and align the fence with it. Remove the scrap and resaw as described below.

Support

To resaw on a band saw, you'll need to support the wood during the cut since it's on its edge. I suggest making a sturdy fence like the one shown in the middle photo. It's two pieces of MDF or plywood screwed together at a right angle, with a pair of triangle-shaped support blocks to provide rigidity and ensure a 90-degree cut. Cutting a notch near the saw's guide assembly lets you lower it when resawing short workpieces. Install a resaw blade, and increase blade tension to at least the next blade width. For instance, if you're using a $3/8$"-wide blade, adjust tension for $1/2$". Then lower the blade guard as close to the workpiece as possible and clamp the fence to the table for the desired cut.

Turn on the saw and guide the workpiece into the blade (*bottom photo*). Use steady, even pressure. Don't force the cut—let the blade do the work. Remember, you're removing a lot of material here—it's slow going. As you complete the cut, use a push block to safely push the workpiece past the saw blade. The most common problem you're likely to encounter while resawing is a bowed cut. A bowed cut (or "barreling") is usually caused by a blade that's not tensioned or supported properly. First, check to make sure the upper guide assembly is as close as possible to the workpiece. If it is, then increase blade tension until it cuts straight.

MITER SAWS

I have to admit that years ago, when the first miter saws (often referred to as chop saws) were introduced, I didn't get too excited. It seemed like they'd be great at a construction site for framers and trim carpenters, but not in a woodworker's shop. When compound miter saws were introduced, I started getting more interested. And when sliding compound miter saws hit the market, I knew I had to have one. I've gone through about six miter saws over the years and really couldn't imagine working without one. Let's take a look at the differences between the three main types—chop saws, compound saws, and sliding compound saws.

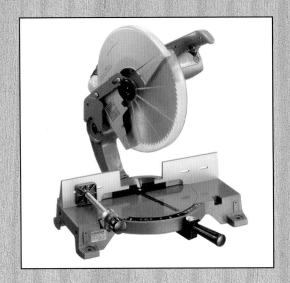

Chop saws

A chop saw (or stand miter saw) gets its name from its action—it chops boards into smaller pieces across their width. Most of these saws are capable of making miter cuts where the saw carriage is rotated to an angle between 0 and 45 degrees—usually in both directions (*top photo*). These saws have limited use but are great for cross-cutting boards to length.

Compound saws

The next step in the evolution of the miter saw was the ability of the blade to tilt—typically only in one direction—anywhere from 0 to 45 degrees (*middle photo*). Couple this with the ability to rotate the blade, and you can cut compound miters (crown molding, look out!). This makes the saw more valuable in the woodworking shop, and for years, this is all I used.

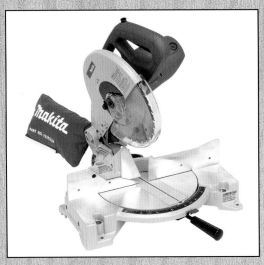

Sliding compound saws

A sliding compound saw offers all the features of the compound saw but has a saw carriage that slides, allowing you to cut wider boards (*bottom photo*). This type of saw has all but replaced the radial arm saw in most woodworking shops—and for good reason. Most have cross-cut capacities of at least 12", they're extremely accurate, and they're portable. What more could you ask for?

Photos courtesy of Makita USA, copyright 2001

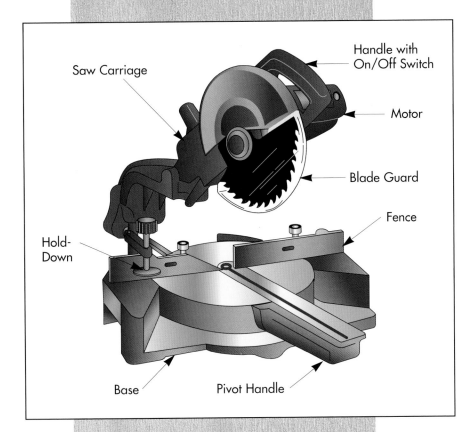

Saw Carriage

Handle with On/Off Switch

Motor

Blade Guard

Fence

Hold-Down

Base

Pivot Handle

Miter saw anatomy

Whether it's a chop saw, compound saw, or sliding compound saw, all miter saws have common parts. They all basically consist of a table with a fence and a saw assembly that pivots up and down to make the cut (*top drawing*).

The saw assembly is made up of the motor, the blade and guard, and the handle and trigger. Depending on the type of saw, there may or may not be locking knobs that allow you to tilt the blade. All models have a knob or handle out front that's used to pivot the saw table for miter cuts. On better-quality saws, the table has a pair of adjustable plastic inserts near the kerf that you can move in or out to match the thickness of the blade. These basically serve as backer boards to help prevent splintering during the cut.

MITER SAW RECOMMENDATIONS

■ If you can afford it, buy a sliding compound miter saw. You won't regret it. I've got a Makita LS1013 that I just love. It's the best miter saw I've ever owned. It cuts amazingly smooth, tilts both ways, and is extremely accurate—but it's not inexpensive. If money is tight, go with a quality compound saw. Look for smooth castings and easy-to-use adjustments. Tilt and rotate the blade to make sure it slides and pivots easily and locks securely in place once the knobs are tightened. Also, be on the lookout for package deals. Manufacturers often sweeten the deals by throwing in extras. A quality carbide-tipped blade is an excellent bonus, as these can easily cost over $100.

MITER SAW FEATURES

In addition to the features listed in the recommendations on page 31, there are a couple of other things to look for when shopping for a miter saw: capacity, miter and bevel capabilities, and hold-downs.

Capacity

The cutting capacity of a miter saw will vary greatly according to the type (*top drawing*). Chop and miter saws can typically cut through a 2×6, in terms of width. The maximum depth of cut will depend on the type of guard that the saw employs. Most saws can handle a 4×4. Sliding compound saws have a greater width capacity, commonly 10" to 12"; check the manufacturer's specifications if you're in doubt.

Miter and bevel cuts

As I mentioned previously, the saw assembly on all miter saws will rotate to handle miter cuts. What you're looking for here is smooth action and a positive lock. The big difference in compound and sliding compound saws is whether or not they tilt in both directions for bevel cuts and how well they move and lock in place (*middle drawing*). Although you may not think it's a big deal, a saw that tilts in both directions can save you headaches from trying to figure out how to make a cut, especially a compound miter.

Hold-downs

Another feature that I look for in a miter saw is built-in hold-downs. These are basically clamps that attach to the fence or body of the saw and are used to press a workpiece flat against the table for a cut (*bottom photo*). This not only adds precision, but also prevents dangerous situations from occurring when either side of a long board that's cut in half tilts up into the spinning blade after a cut is made. Unless you've got three hands, you can't hold down both pieces and make the cut at the same time—thank goodness for hold-downs.

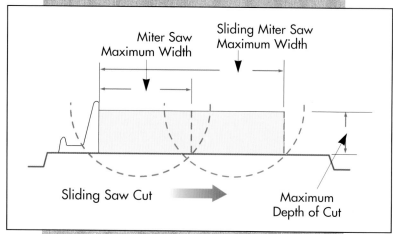

Miter Saw Maximum Width   Sliding Miter Saw Maximum Width

Sliding Saw Cut   Maximum Depth of Cut

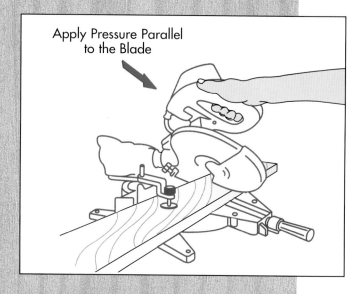

Apply Pressure Parallel to the Blade

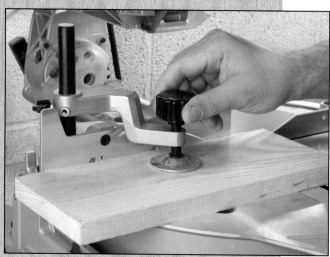

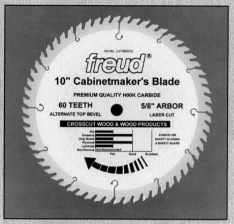

Photo courtesy of Freud Inc., copyright 2001

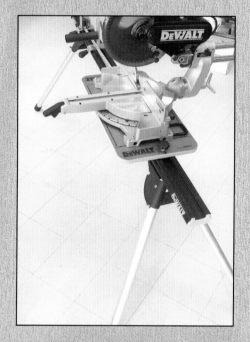

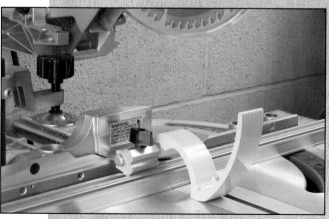

MITER SAW ACCESSORIES

There are a number of accessories for the miter saw that can really improve its performance. These include blades, stands, and after-market fences.

Blades

The HSS blade that comes standard on most miter saws is good only for making a shop clock. Toss it, and buy a quality carbide-tipped blade. For cross-cutting, I recommend a 60-tooth ATB carbide-tipped blade (*top photo*). Yes, it'll cost around $100, but as long as you keep it away from metal fasteners, it'll last a long, long time. With this in mind, I don't recommend cutting used lumber with this blade—or with this saw, for that matter. Put a demolition blade on your circular saw, and use that instead.

Stands

Although I've mounted my miter saw on an old kitchen counter that I have in the shop (it works quite nice), it doesn't help much when I need to use the saw on-site. A number of tool manufacturers make stands for miter saws (*middle photo*). These range from simple fold-up stands to elaborate units with built-in fences and stops, like the one shown here. Costs range from $150 to over $300. If you do a lot of on-site work, one of these may be a good investment. If not, you can always clamp the saw to a sawhorse.

After-market fences

Here's a nice accessory that's well worth the money: an after-market fence for the miter gauge that attaches to the saw's fence and has a slot for an adjustable stop (*bottom photo*). If your miter saw is accurate, one of these can make repeat cuts a snap. A poor man's version (*see page 35*) is to attach a strip of wood to the fence and clamp on a wood stop block. This works fine, but the extruded fence shown here is a lot handier.

MITER SAW: CROSS CUTS

Even though a miter saw excels at handling miter cuts, I'd have to say that about 80% of the cuts I make with my miter saw are 90-degree cross cuts for breaking down long boards into more-manageable pieces or making finish cuts to length. Although the basic operation of a miter saw is straightforward, there are a number of things you can do to make your cuts more precise, including using an insert, checking the blade alignment, and using a fence.

Adjustable inserts

If your saw has built-in adjustable inserts like those shown in the top photo, take the time to adjust them to snug up against the saw blade. These inserts serve as backer boards to back up the workpiece as the blade exits the piece. Without them, the stock will splinter. If your saw doesn't have these, you can affix a piece of 1/4" hardboard to the table with double-sided tape. Then just cut through this when you cut the workpiece. Note: Make sure to open up and readjust the inserts when you tilt the blade for a bevel cut, or you'll end up cutting into them.

Blade alignment

It's a good idea to check your blade alignment on a routine basis, particularly before making finish cuts. I use a small engineer's square and place it on the table so the long blade butts up against the saw blade (*middle photo*). If it's not perfectly flush, loosen the blade-tilt knob and adjust as necessary. Even if your 90-degree stop is set accurately, sawdust can get in the way to foul things up. It's always worth your time to make this quick check.

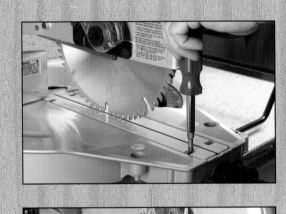

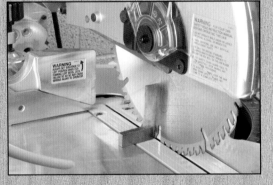

SLIDING CUTS

All sliding-saw manufacturers describe the sequence for using their saws as follows: With the saw off, slide the carriage out past the edge of the workpiece; then turn on the saw and pivot the blade down—then slide the carriage back toward the fence to make the cut (*bottom drawing*). If you think about it, this is how you'd make the cut with a circular saw. If you did it the other way, the saw could grab the wood and "run." This is one reason that there's a safety recall on most radial arm saws.

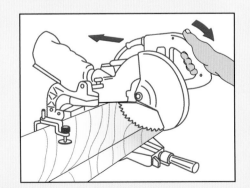

An auxiliary fence

Another inaccuracy on the miter saw can be caused by cutting long boards using the short fence that's built into the saw. These fences are fine for short boards, but a long board can easily shift or pivot during the cut. To prevent this, I always attach a longer fence to the saw's fence. Using plywood or a known-straight hardwood board, secure the fence to both sides of the saw fence with screws (*top photo*). Note that this will decrease your maximum width of cut by the thickness of the auxiliary fence—but you can remove the fence if you need the extra $3/4$".

Add stops for repeat cuts

A side benefit of adding an auxiliary fence like the one described above is that you can attach a stop block to the fence to make accurate repeat cuts (*middle photo*). Just make sure to clamp the stop to the fence so it's perpendicular to the saw table and that it's clamped securely. ShopTip: Apply a strip of sandpaper to the backside of the stop—this will help it grip the fence better when it's clamped in place.

PREVENTING "CREEP"

Even if your saw is properly aligned, chances are that you'll occasionally notice that your cuts are not perfectly square on the ends. The problem may not be the saw; the culprit is often the wood itself. Since the grain and density of wood varies from piece to piece and even within a piece, the saw blade can struggle to cut through the denser wood (often a knot, or near a knot). When this happens, the blade can shift the workpiece slightly during the cut. This is known as "creep" and can be prevented a couple

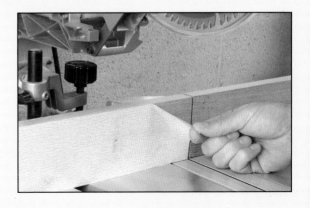

of ways. First, if you saw has a hold-down, use it. If it doesn't consider adding a strip of sandpaper to the saw's fence (*bottom photo*). The sandpaper grit grips the wood and helps prevent it from creeping.

MITER SAW: ANGLES

Rotate for miters

How well your miter saw accurately cuts miters will depend a lot on how well the pivoting system was designed and how precise the graduations are. For the most part, I don't trust built-in graduations until I've checked them and made any compensating adjustments. I suggest rotating the saw to 45 degrees and making a pair of cuts on two scraps (*top photo*). Hold the pieces together at the miter and check to see whether they combine to make a 90-degree corner. Adjust the stops as necessary until they do.

Note: It's important to keep the pivoting mechanism as clean as possible. If bits of dust and dirt sneak in between the two pivoting surfaces, it can abrade the plates and even cause them to lock up. I discovered this the hard way and snapped the pivot handle off my first saw when it seized up as I was pivoting it.

Tilt for bevels

I feel the same way about tilting the blade as I do about rotating it—don't trust the graduations until you've checked their accuracy (*middle photo*). Here again, I'd suggest making a pair of 45-degree bevel cuts and check to see whether they form a 90-degree corner. Adjust the stop as necessary; consult your owner's manual for adjustment procedure. Also, make sure to support the saw carriage with one hand as you tilt it. They're heavy, and gravity will cause them to slam into the stop if you don't support the carriage before you loosen the locking knob.

Increasing accuracy

Here's a trick that I learned from a trim carpenter that's particularly useful when you're making compound cuts. It's often a lot easier to hold the work-

piece at the desired angle (say, 45 degrees) and then just rotate the saw to make the cut. The challenge is keeping the workpiece from shifting during the cut. My carpenter pal just clamps a scrap of wood onto the saw table at the desired distance from the saw fence (*bottom photo*). This both holds the piece at the correct angle and prevents it from moving.

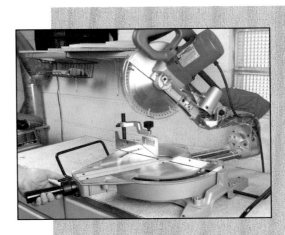

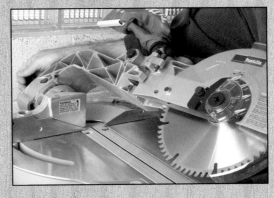

Photo courtesy of Makita USA, copyright 2001

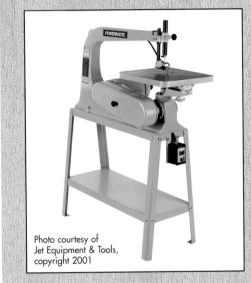

Photo courtesy of
Jet Equipment & Tools,
copyright 2001

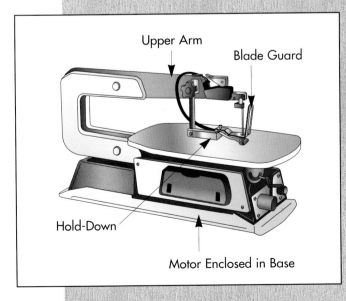

Upper Arm

Blade Guard

Hold-Down

Motor Enclosed in Base

SCROLL SAWS

I've always felt that scroll saws are an underrated shop tool. They have a reputation for use only to make fancy scrollwork: silhouettes, puzzles, etc. And although I occasionally do this type of work, I use my scroll saw regularly on all types of projects. There are two reason for this. First, a scroll saw can make pierced cuts (cuts in from the edge of a workpiece)—something a band saw can't handle. Second, with the proper blade, the cut left by a scroll saw is amazingly smooth. Combine these and you have a tool that can solve a lot of problems. There are two main types of scroll saws: bench-top and stationary.

Bench-top

Bench-top scroll saws are perfect for shops with space limitations (*top photo*). They can handle a wide variety of work and are lightweight enough for easy storage. Most of these can handle stock up to 2" in thickness and have throat capacities typically around 16". The table generally tilts for bevel cuts, and the saw may or may not have variable speeds.

Stationary

Stationary scroll saws are beefier versions of the bench-top saws (*middle photo*). They come with a stand and have heavier castings and typically larger throat capacities, as well as being able to handle thicker stock. The stand provides a stable platform for the saw, but it also takes up floor space in the shop. This type of saw is for serious scroll saw enthusiasts.

Anatomy

Bench-top and stationary scroll saws have similar parts. The removable blade of the saw is held in place by clamps on the top and bottom arms of the saw (*bottom drawing*). The motor is enclosed in the saw housing and drives the lower arm up and down to move the blade. An adjustable hold-down attaches to the top arm and is used to keep the workpiece from chattering. Attached to the hold-down is an adjustable guard to keep fingers away from the blade.

Scroll Saw Features

There are a number of features to look for when shopping for a scroll saw: quick blade change, a reliable blower, and variable speeds.

Quick blade change

Whoever invented the quick blade change mechanism for scroll saws deserves a medal. I've used older scroll saws where changing blades is frustrating and can easily take 10 minutes. With the new quick-clamp mechanisms, I can change a blade in about 30 seconds—without pulling my hair. In my opinion this is absolutely a necessity. The bottom of the blade is clamped in place with an Allen screw that's easy to loosen and tighten with the self-aligning wrench. The top of the blade is secured via a clamp that opens and closes with the touch of a finger (*top left photo*). Fabulous!

Blower

Most scroll saws come with a built-in blower to keep sawdust from obscuring the cut line. Make sure that the blower is heavy-duty and that the air is conveyed to the upper arm in a reliable way. Plastic tubing like that shown in the top right photo tends to kink with use, shutting off the airflow. I recommend purchasing a spare blower pump and tubing when you buy your saw. They'll both eventually wear out, and you'll be glad you have the spare parts on hand when that happens.

Variable speed

Variable speed is a nice feature that lets you match the speed to the material you're cutting. This is especially useful with non-wood materials, like plastic and brass. Most saws have at least a low and a high speed (*middle photo*), while more deluxe versions offer continuously variable speed.

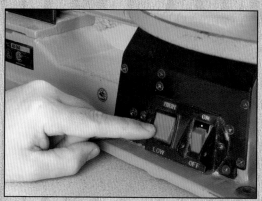

SCROLL SAW RECOMMENDATIONS

If you've got plenty of shop space and plan to do a lot of scrollwork, I'd suggest a stationary scroll saw. If shop space is at a premium, a smaller bench-top model will serve you well. Some of the bench-top models out there rival the stability and performance of their larger stationary cousins. Look for a quick blade-change mechanism and a saw that runs smoothly with minimal vibration.

SCROLL SAW ACCESSORIES

There are two basic types of scroll saw blades available: plain-end and pin-end. The most common type is the plain-end (*top photo*).

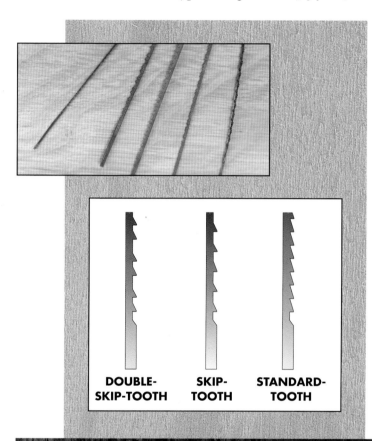

DOUBLE-SKIP-TOOTH **SKIP-TOOTH** **STANDARD-TOOTH**

This blade slips into slotted clamp heads, and then a screw or clamp is tightened to grip the blade. Pin-end blades were common on older machines and have metal pins welded to the top and bottom of the blade to fit into U-shaped clips on the saw arms.

Styles

Both types of blades come in different styles, with the plain-end type having the greater variety. You'll find there are three basic styles to choose from: standard-tooth, skip-tooth, and double-skip-tooth (*middle drawing*). For years, the only type of scroll saw blades you could buy were the traditional standard-tooth blade, which has evenly spaced teeth along the length of the blade. The next step in the evolution of the scroll blade was to remove every other tooth to create a skip-tooth blade, where the deeper gullet efficiently removes sawdust from the kerf. This keeps the blade cooler, prolonging its life. The double-skip-tooth blade is similar to the skip-tooth except that it has two teeth in a row, skip one, and so on. This provides a smoother cut but does not allow you to cut as fast as when using a skip-tooth blade.

Specialty blades

There are two specialty blades that have found wide acceptance with scroll sawyers: reverse-tooth and spiral blades. On reverse-tooth blades, the last few teeth near the bottom of the blade are reversed. This reduces splintering but should not be used with thin stock since the reversed teeth tend to lift the workpiece during the cut. Spiral blades are scroll saw blades that are twisted so the teeth point in different directions. This means that you can saw in any direction without turning the workpiece. Their disadvantage is that they create a wide kerf and tend to follow the grain, which makes it difficult to follow a cut line.

PRECISION BLADES

Although precision blades appear similar to skip-tooth blades, there's one important difference. Instead of the teeth being stamped out, the teeth on these blades are ground with a grinding wheel. This creates

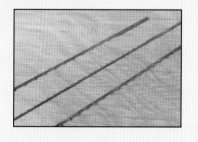

super-sharp teeth that cut easily through most stock. They're available from Advanced Machinery Imports at www.advmachinery.com.

PATTERN CUTTING

The vast majority of the cutting you do on a scroll saw will be pattern cutting, where you're following a pattern or a line drawn directly on the workpiece.

Since that's what these saws do so well, it's just a matter of setting up the saw and cutting. Consult your owner's manual for the correct procedure to install the desired blade.

Adjust tension

Once the blade is installed, you can adjust the tension. On most saws this is accomplished by turning a knob on either the front or rear of the top arm (*top photo*). Since most saws don't have any kind of tension indicator, you'll have to find the right tension by trial and error. If the tension is too high, you'll find that you'll break a lot of blades. Too loose and the blade can bow, creating a "barrel" cut. Over the years, I've learned to tell the right tension by sound: I pluck the blade and tweak the tension until it sounds right. You'll have to experiment to find your right "note."

Adjust hold-down

The final step before beginning work is to adjust the position of the hold-down. With most saws the hold-down is a piece of spring steel that flexes to help press the workpiece firmly against the saw's table. To prevent the workpiece from chattering during the cut, lower the hold-down until it touches the workpiece and then lower it a tad more to put some tension on it (*middle photo*). Lock the hold-down knob, and check to make sure you can still slide the workpiece under the hold-down without having to use undue force.

SPRAY ADHESIVE

One of the simplest ways to cut out a pattern is to attach the pattern directly to the workpiece with spray adhesive (*bottom photo*). I've used rubber cement before, but it doesn't have the holding power of spray adhesive. Apply a coat or two to the back of the pattern, and simply press it in place. Note: You can remove residual adhesive using lacquer thinner once you've peeled off the pattern.

Basic technique

Select the correct speed to match your material, and turn on the saw. Note: If your saw is a bench-top model, secure it to the bench with

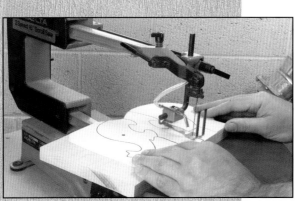

clamps—even the finest bench-top saw will vibrate some, and the last thing you want is a running saw in your lap. Get comfortable (I usually sit on my shop stool), and gently push the workpiece into the blade (*top photo*). The biggest mistake I see beginning sawyers make is that they tend to push the stock too fast. Let the blade do the work. If you notice that the blade is bowing, it's a sure sign that you're feeding the stock too fast, or you've got the wrong blade or speed for the job. Slow the feed rate down as you approach tight curves, and again, let the blade do the work. If you relax and you're patient (as you need to be with fancy scrollwork), you'll find scrollwork both satisfying and rewarding.

PIERCED CUTS

As I mentioned earlier, pierced cuts are one of the most common reasons why I reach for my scroll saw. A pierced cut is any cut that's in from the edge of a workpiece—that is, the blade does not enter via a kerf. Instead the blade is detached from one arm of the scroll saw (usually the top one, as this is where a quick blade-change clamp will be), and the blade is threaded through a starter hole drilled into the wood. The blade is then reattached to the top arm, tension is applied, and the cut is made (*photo and drawing at right*).

A couple of tips here. First, drill lots of starter holes—they're free, and they'll make it easier to make a pierced cut. I tend to drill a hole in every corner and anywhere where it looks like it'll be tough to make a turn. Second, stop the saw every time you cut off a piece of waste. Remove the waste piece and continue. If you leave it in place, it'll tend to catch the blade and will either jam or snap the blade. It's worth the three seconds it takes to do this. Finally, make sure you've got a lot of good light pointed at the table. Pierced work can be intricate at times and quite fatiguing to your eyes if the lighting is inadequate.

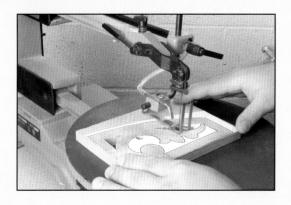

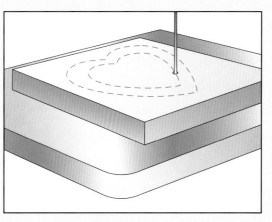

CIRCULAR SAWS

There are two basic flavors of circular saw: shaft-drive and worm-drive. By far the most common homeowner saw is the shaft-drive, but the worm-drive type is favored in construction because of its ruggedness and ease of use.

Shaft-drive

Shaft-drive saws are popular because they're relatively inexpensive. You can buy one for less than $30, or spend up to $150 for a quality saw. Regardless of the quality, they all use the motor's shaft to directly drive the blade (*top photo*). For the average woodworker, this type of saw is just fine. Stay away from the bargain-store varieties, and buy a name you can trust. You'd be amazed at the difference between a $30 saw and a $60 saw. The $60 saw will have better castings and beefier parts and will be manufactured to closer tolerances, resulting in a more accurate cut.

Worm-drive

My shop saw is a worm-drive. Yes, it cost more, but it's worth it. In addition to being rugged and well-built, I find that a worm-drive saw is much easier to make accurate cuts with (*middle photo*). That's because the motor is in line with my arm—it's a more natural motion, and the saw tends to almost guide itself in a straight line. Note: As these are industrial-strength saws, they tend to weigh a lot—and some people aren't comfortable with this. Make sure to visit a tool store and try a one-handed cut with one of these before you buy.

Anatomy

The saw blade attaches to an arbor that is either the motor shaft or a gear box (as with a worm-drive saw). A pivoting blade guard retracts up and out of the way during the cut and slips back down to cover the exposed blade once the cut is made. The base of the saw pivots from side to side for bevel cuts and from front to back to adjust the depth of cut. The trigger is housed in the handle. Look for easy-to-use adjustments and quality castings.

Photo courtesy of
Makita USA, copyright 2001

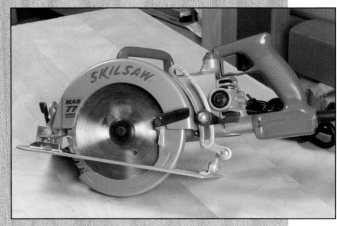

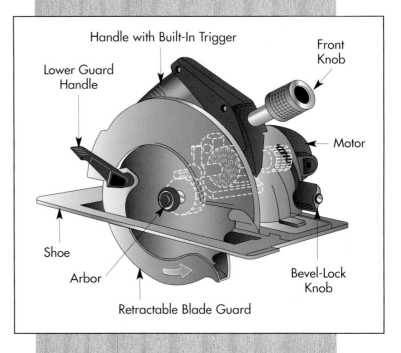

Handle with Built-In Trigger

Front Knob

Lower Guard Handle

Motor

Shoe

Bevel-Lock Knob

Arbor

Retractable Blade Guard

Photo courtesy of Freud Inc., copyright 2001

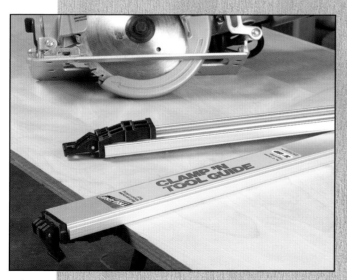

CIRCULAR SAW ACCESSORIES

Blades

The most common accessories for circular saws are blades (*top photo*). They come in a dizzying variety of shapes, sizes, and features. I recommend buying carbide-tipped blades. They stay sharper longer and don't cost a whole lot more. For general-purpose work, stick with a combination blade. Although this style of blade excels at neither ripping nor cross-cutting, it handles both tasks well—and you don't have to change blades when switching between the two. Unless you're dealing with expensive wood or plywood, where loss of wood from the saw's kerf is a big deal, avoid thin-kerf blades—they tend to vibrate excessively and can produce inaccurate cuts, particularly in thicker stock.

Fences

Another common accessory for the circular saw is a fence (*middle photo*). This is just a T-shaped bar that slips into the saw base. It's held in place via a knurled knob or wing nut. Look for a fence that's made of thick bar stock and is rigid. Check the locking mechanism to make sure it holds the fence securely in place. Better-quality fences will have a large metal fence face that also allows you to attach a wood auxiliary fence for added stability.

Guides

Clamp-on straightedges are great for making long cuts with accuracy (*bottom photo*). They clamp on to the edges of the workpiece, and because of their low-profile, the saw can pass directly over them to make the cut. For short, straight cuts, I use a speed square. A speed square is a metal layout tool that's basically a right triangle. A lip on one edge makes it easy to use to mark stock for square or mitered cuts. Just butt the saw up against the edge of the speed square and slide it over so that the blade aligns with the marked line; then make the cut.

CIRCULAR SAW TECHNIQUES

Depth of cut

As long as you're making a straight cut, about the only adjustment you'll need to make on a circular saw before using it is to adjust the depth of cut. Some folks leave their saw set for the maximum cut and use this for all cuts. This is unsafe and can also produce a jagged cut. Most saw manufacturers recommend that you adjust the saw so that one full tooth of the saw blade extends past the surface of the workpiece (*top drawing*). This minimizes the amount of exposed blade while allowing the gullets between the teeth plenty of clearance to empty chips. It also creates more of a shearing action to produce a cleaner cut and reduces splintering.

Cutting plywood

Because it's constructed of several thin layers of veneer, plywood can be a challenge to cut smoothly with a circular saw. Even if you use a special plywood blade with many small teeth, the thin outer layer (or face veneer) can and will tear (*middle drawing*). To protect the "good" face of the plywood, always cut the plywood with good face down, as shown in the middle drawing. This doesn't prevent splintering—it just happens on the unseen back of the plywood. If both faces will be seen, score the face veneer with a utility knife along the cut line to reduce the chances of splintering.

Cross cuts

The most common cut you'll make with a circular saw is the cross cut. This is where you're cutting across the grain, such as when trimming a board to length. Place the saw on the workpiece, and align the blade so it's on the waste side of the marked line. Depress the trigger and push the saw into the workpiece. Continue with one smooth motion to cut through the entire piece. For added accuracy, use a speed square to guide the saw. Just place it on the workpiece so

the lip of the square catches the edge of the workpiece (*bottom photo*). Butt the saw up against the adjacent edge of the square, and slide the saw and square so the blade is on the waste side of the marked line. Then holding the square firmly in place, depress the trigger and push the saw through the cut, keeping the saw base in constant contact with the square.

One Tooth Length Should Be Exposed to Minimize Splintering

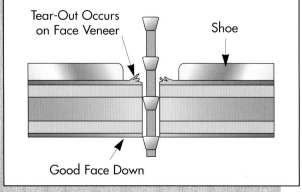

Tear-Out Occurs on Face Veneer

Shoe

Good Face Down

Rip cuts

Occasionally, you'll need to trim or "rip" a board to width with a circular saw. This type of cut is made along the grain and is best accomplished with the aid of a fence (*top photo*). Slide the bar into the appropriate slots in the base of the saw, and adjust its position for the desired width of cut. Lock the fence in place with the clamp provided, and place the saw on the workpiece with the edge of the fence pressing against the workpiece. Depress the trigger and make the cut, taking care to keep the fence in constant contact with the edge of the workpiece as you cut.

Sheet stock

Depending on your project, you may need to break down sheet stock into more manageable-sized pieces with the circular saw before cutting them to final size with a table saw. The most accurate way to cut sheets is to use a shop-made or commercial straightedge like the one shown in the middle photo. Set the sheet stock on a pair of sawhorses, position the straightedge so the saw blade is on the waste side of the marked line, and clamp it in place. To make the cut, press the edge of the saw base firmly against the straightedge over the full length of the cut.

Plunge cut

Square cutouts in sheet stock can be made by taking a "plunge" cut with a circular saw (*bottom photo*). To make a plunge cut, position the saw so the blade is on the waste side of the cutout. Hold the front of the saw base against the workpiece and tilt the saw as shown. Retract the blade guard to expose the blade, and depress the trigger. Slowly lower the saw to plunge the blade into the workpiece. Move the saw forward, stopping before you reach the marked line. Do this for all four sides, and then use a handsaw to complete the cuts in the corners.

WORKING WITH SHEET STOCK

One of the main reasons I reach for my circular saw in the shop is to break down sheets of plywood into manageable pieces for the table saw. (In days past, I had to do this just to get the pieces into my shop, it was so small.) Regardless of whether you're breaking down plywood or making the final cuts, here are a couple of tips that can add accuracy to the job.

Rigid foam

Perhaps the largest challenge of cutting plywood is the awkward size of the sheets. They're just too big for the average person to comfortably toss around the shop. A nifty way to get around this is to lay the sheet flat on the ground on top of a sheet of rigid foam insulation (*top photo*). I keep a couple sheets of this around the shop just for this purpose. Foam insulation like this is inexpensive, and lightweight as well. Set your saw to just cut through your workpiece, and make the cut. The blade will pass through the workpiece and will score the foam. You can do this a lot before the foam gets chewed up and you need a new piece. In addition to fully supporting the sheet stock over its entire length and width, backing up the cut like this also reduces splintering. This technique works especially well for thin sheets that tend to flex a lot.

Cleats

Another way to support sheets for cutting is to set the sheet stock on 2-by cleats resting on a sawhorse. Just make sure to support both sides of the cut as shown in the middle drawing. The big advantage of this technique is that it raises the workpiece up off the floor so you don't have to bend over or crawl along on your knees. Here again, if the stock is thin, consider backing it up with a layer of rigid foam board.

Straightedges

Even if you're good with a circular saw, odds are that you can use a little help when making a full-length cut along a sheet (*bottom photo*). I keep a known-straight piece of 8-foot-long wood around the shop just for this purpose. You can either clamp the straightedge to the edges of the workpiece to guide the cut, or attach it with double-sided carpet tape.

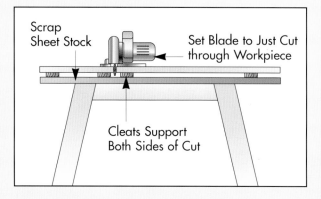

Scrap Sheet Stock

Set Blade to Just Cut through Workpiece

Cleats Support Both Sides of Cut

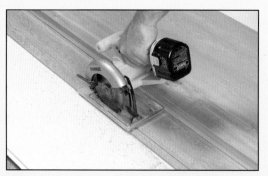

SABER SAWS

There are two basic types of saber saws (commonly referred to as jigsaws) on the market: standard saws and orbital saws. I used a standard saw for years, and when I made the jump to an orbital saw, I wished that I'd done it much earlier.

Standard

Standard saber saws can be purchased at bargain stores for less than $30. You can also buy a higher-quality standard saw for upwards of $100, but I'd recommend spending a little bit extra to buy an orbital saw (*top photo*). Besides not offering orbital action (*see below*), standard saws commonly don't offer variable speeds (a necessity) and often aren't as rugged as their orbital cousins.

Orbital

A quality orbital saber saw is a joy to use—really. There's a huge difference between one of these and an inexpensive standard saber saw. The orbital feature (*see page* 48) offers quicker, more aggressive cuts, especially in thicker woods. Orbital saber saws tend to be made with thicker castings, better bearings, and higher tolerances (*middle photo*). They are virtually vibration-free, and they cut through most materials like butter.

Anatomy

The saber saw is a simple tool that, if maintained properly, can last a lifetime. Most saber saws have the motor in line with the handle, and the up-and-down action is accomplished via an internal gear box (*bottom drawing*). The trigger is typically housed in the handle and may have an integral speed adjustment. The base on most saber saws tilts for beveled cuts and usually is designed to accept a rip fence. Quality saber saws will feature heavy-duty castings, variable speed, and orbital action.

Photo courtesy of Makita USA, copyright 2001

Photo courtesy of Freud Inc., copyright 2001

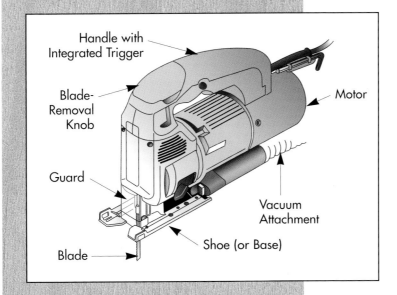

Handle with Integrated Trigger

Blade-Removal Knob

Guard

Blade

Motor

Vacuum Attachment

Shoe (or Base)

Saber Saw Features

Variable speed

One feature that's a must-have for a saber saw is variable speed. Being able to adjust the speed allows you to match the saw's speed to the type of material you're cutting. This is particularly important when cutting into metals and other non-wood materials. It's also nice to be able to slow down a cut for added accuracy. On some saber saws, the speed adjustment is a wheel on the top of the saw casing. Others (like the one shown in the top photo) incorporate this into the trigger mechanism—this allows for one-handed speed adjustment.

Orbital blade

Another feature that I recommend in a saber saw is an orbital blade. Most saber saws with this feature offer three to four ranges, including an OFF position (*middle drawing*). In the OFF position, the blade cuts straight up and down. As the orbital action is increased, the blade begins to pivot out during the cut. This pivoting, or orbital action, creates a much more aggressive cut. The greater the orbital action, the quicker you can chew through wood. This is great for rough cuts but should be turned off when you need a smooth cut, or when cutting plywood (the orbital action tends to tear up the face veneer).

Blade changing

Although blade changing may not seem like a big deal in a saber saw, it can have a big impact on the quality of your work. If changing the blade is a chore, you'll often avoid this and continue working with a dull blade. An easy-to-use system (like the no-tools-required system shown

in the bottom photo) increases the likelihood that you'll change the blade more often. Look for a system that is quick and that locks the blade securely in place.

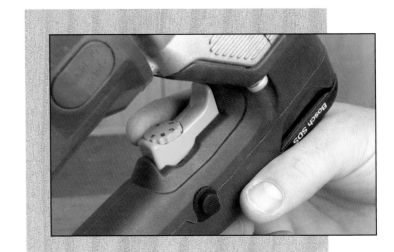

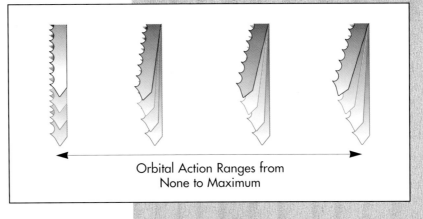

Orbital Action Ranges from
None to Maximum

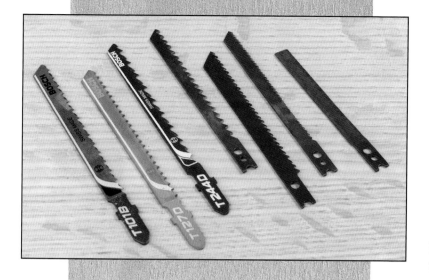

Saber Saw Accessories

Just as with the circular saw, the number one accessories for saber saws are blades (*top photo*). Regardless of the size and shape, most saber saw blades have one of two types of shanks: bayonet or universal. The bayonet-style shank (blades at left in top photo) look like the handle of a bayonet or sword. These are common on more expensive saber saws, and they reliably lock in place. The universal-style shank (blades at right in top photo) have one or two holes in the shank, where a screw or dimpled metal plate engages to hold the blade in place.

Profiles

The profile and tooth configuration of a blade will define its use (*middle drawing*). Small, fine teeth are used when cutting metal, and larger, coarse teeth are designed to handle wood. Most blades are made from high-speed steel (HSS) and are fine for general-purpose work. Scroll-cut blades have narrower bodies and finer teeth for smooth cuts in tight turns in wood. Higher-quality blades are often bi-metal and have a tendency to hold up longer when worked hard (but at a cost—they're often twice as much as a HSS blade). There's even carbide-coated blades for cutting into tile and other composite materials.

Rip fence

Most quality saber saws are designed to accept a rip fence (*bottom photo*). These are great for making straight narrow rips—particularly for accurately cutting notches or openings in sheet stock. A nice feature of the rip fence shown here is that it comes with a detachable metal pivot point that converts the rip fence into a circle cutter. Just snap the pivot point in place, set the fence, and cut a perfect circle.

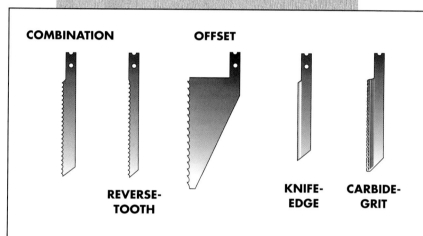

COMBINATION OFFSET REVERSE-TOOTH KNIFE-EDGE CARBIDE-GRIT

SABER SAW CUTS

Starter hole

The main reason I reach for a saber saw in my shop is to make a pierced cut—that is, a cut that's in from the edge of the workpiece. Although you can start by making a plunge cut (*see page 51*), you'll find it easier to first drill a starter hole for the blade (*top photo*). I tend to use a ³/₈" brad-point bit since this accepts most blades I use and tends to cut a clean hole with minimum chipout. You'll also find that it's easiest to drill a hole inside every corner. This allows you to pivot the blade easily when cutting adjacent sides. After the opening has been cut out, you can go back and square up the corners with the saw. ShopTip: Since most blades are up-cutting, the good face of the workpiece should be down. With this in mind, it's best to use a backer board when drilling the holes, to prevent tear-out on the good side (*see page 66 for more on backer boards*).

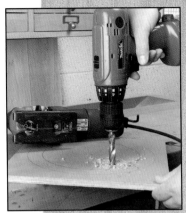

Straight cuts

For straight rough cuts with a saber saw, just position the blade on the waste side of the cut line and make the cut (*middle photo*). Keeping your shoulder, arm, and elbow in line with the saw and cut line will increase the chances of a straight cut. For added accuracy, clamp a straightedge to the workpiece to guide the saw.

PREVENTING TEAR-OUT

If you're making a cut where both faces of the workpiece need to be smooth, use one of these tips to reduce tear-out. A simple way to support the thin face veneer is to run a layer of masking tape directly over the cut line (you'll need to redraw this on the tape). Then make your cut as usual (*top photo at left*). When done, carefully peel off the tape. An even more reliable method is to score through the face veneer with a utility knife (*bottom photo at left*). As long as your blade stays on the waste side of the scored line, the resulting cut will be smooth.

Curved cuts

For folks without a band saw or a scroll saw, the saber saw is their number one curve-cutting tool. I know for years it was all I had. Just as with a band saw (*see page 25*), the width of the blade will determine how tight of a radius you can cut (*top photo*). Some manufacturers sell "scroll saw" blades for saber saws. Although this naming convention is a bit confusing, these are just standard saber saw blades that are narrower and can be used to cut tighter curves. A word of warning about "scroll saw" saber saw blades: Since they're narrow, they tend to deflect easily. If you use them, make cuts only in stock that's 3/4" or thinner, take your time, and don't use the orbital feature.

Orbiting cuts

Orbiting action is best used for straight cuts when you want to remove a lot of wood in a hurry. Because the blade pivots or orbits out during the stroke, it can create undue stress on the blade if you make a curved cut. This is less of a concern for large-radius or gentle curves, but it comes into play for tight curves. In addition to taking a more aggressive cut, the orbiting action also better clears out sawdust from the blade gullets and kerf. This helps keep the blade cooler and will extend its cutting life.

Plunge cuts

I don't make a lot of plunge cuts with a saber saw, since I tend to use my circular saw for this. There are occasions, however, where it is the best tool for the job, such as for the narrow slot being cut in the bottom photo. The slot is too narrow for a starter hole, so a plunge cut is used. The technique is the same as that used for a circular saw (*see page 45*). Just make sure to turn off the orbital action because this makes it extremely difficult to start the cut.

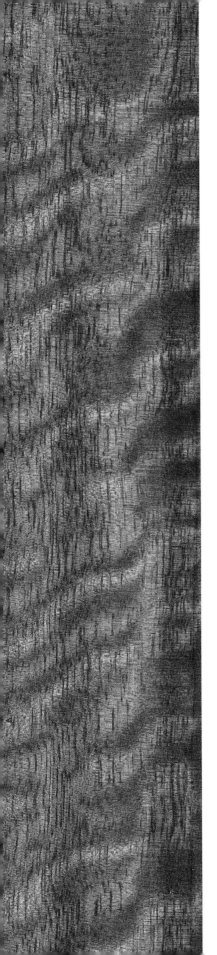

DRILLS and DRILL PRESSES

As Mr. Stickley aptly notes, drilling holes in wood does not leave a lot of room for creativity. It may not be an exciting chore, but it certainly needs to be exacting—and that's where portable drills and drill presses come in.

For the average woodworking project, it's surprising how critical hole placement can be. In many cases, holes are drilled for hardware used to assemble the project. There is rarely room for "close enough": If there's any inaccuracy here, it doesn't matter how tight-fitting your joints are, or how straight and true your lumber is. If the holes you drill to mount a hinged door on a case are crooked, you've wasted time and materials. The same goes for holes drilled for joinery and construction, such as mortises or holes that define the ends of a slot.

That said, there's more to drilling a hole than chucking up a bit in a power drill and boring. To achieve precision, you need to know what bit is best for the job, what speed and feed rate to use, and how to hold the work or the drill for an accurate hole.

Before double-insulated tools appeared, most portable power tools had metal casings for ruggedness, like the two Craftsman drills shown here. *At top,* a ³⁄₈" electric drill, model number 315.11150, with speed torque control; *at the bottom,* a D-handled ¹⁄₄" electric drill, model number 315.2578.

PORTABLE DRILLS

Portable drills are manufactured in more styles, shapes, and sizes than any other portable electric tool. Portable drills are categorized as being either cordless or corded. There's no doubt about it, using a cordless drill is habit-forming (*top photo*). No more getting tangled in extension cords, or losing power because you stretched the cord and pulled out the plug. There are also safety advantages: no power cords to accidentally fall in a puddle of water, no cords to catch on protrusions when working on a ladder and cause you to lose your balance, and so forth.

OK, if a cordless drill is so convenient, then why would I even consider a corded version? The answer is power. On a corded drill, you have unlimited power as long as you stay plugged in; there are no batteries to swap when they run down. This is a particular nuisance for sustained-power or high-torque jobs. By this I mean mixing a bucket of drywall mud (*middle photo*), drilling a series of holes in concrete, or driving deck screws— most cordless drills just couldn't keep up.

Another feature corded drills offer over their cordless cousins is a power lock. A power lock allows you to "lock" the trigger in the ON position. This may not seem like a big deal, but it is if you're mixing paint, grinding, sanding, or polishing. A power lock also frees up your hands if you're using either a horizontal or vertical drill stand.

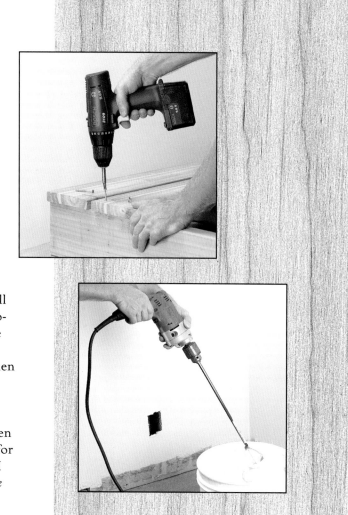

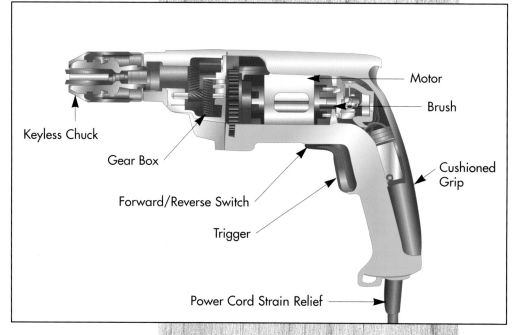

Keyless Chuck

Gear Box

Forward/Reverse Switch

Trigger

Power Cord Strain Relief

Motor

Brush

Cushioned Grip

PORTABLE DRILL FEATURES

Batteries and charging systems

One of the best indicators of a cordless drill's power capabilities is its battery size. The higher the voltage, generally the more powerful the drill. Likewise, higher-voltage batteries usually provide greater torque. The charging system will also affect a cordless drill's performance (*top photo*). Charging times vary from overnight to 15 minutes, but most systems recharge in a couple hours. Unless you absolutely need to recharge a battery over a coffee break, stay away from 15-minute chargers. Since they charge so quickly, these systems tend to overheat the battery, which will shorten its life.

Clutch

A much-hyped and often misunderstood feature of a cordless drill is a clutch for driving screws. In the middle photo, the top drill has no clutch; the lower drill does (note the plastic collar by the chuck). When the drill is in "drive" mode and the desired torque is achieved, the clutch slips and the bit stops turning. In keeping with the "more is better" philosophy, tool manufacturers offer drills with up to 25 clutch settings. In my experience, a dozen settings is plenty; any more and you'll spend too much time trying to find the "perfect" setting.

Motor ratings and speeds

Although toolmakers use various descriptors to indicate the "power" of a drill, the true indicator is its amperage rating (*bottom photo*). In general, the higher the amperage, the more powerful the drill. Drill speeds and ranges also affect "power." In most cases, the lower the speed, the higher the torque. Speed ranges for drills vary from 0–500 rpm up to 0–2,500 rpm, often with two ranges so you can select between high-torque/low-speed and low-torque/high-speed to match your application; cordless drills with both ranges are called "driver/drills."

Even after assessing all the various features, there's no substitute for picking up a drill to see how it fits in your hand. How is the balance? Are the controls accessible? Does it feel right? These are questions that only you can answer. I've seen plenty of folks change their mind about a drill by just picking it up. Drills are configured in one of two ways: pistol-grip or T-handle. Virtually all corded drills are pistol-grip. Cordless drills can be either.

Grips

The T-handle design evolved as batteries for cordless drills got larger and heavier; coupling a large, heavy battery with a traditional pistol-grip made the drill tip off-center. So tool manufacturers positioned the weight closer to center, creating a "T" (*top photo*). This balanced the drill so well that the T-handle has become the preferred configuration in cordless drills. Although you may find T-handle drills better balanced, the handle in the center can prevent you from exerting direct force in line with the bit. Since many drilling tasks need to be done with one hand, a pistol-grip drill (*inset photo*) lets you get your weight behind the drill.

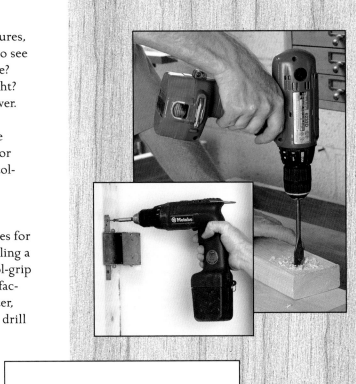

Chucks

All chucks work on the same principle—a set of jaws inside the chuck housing move up and down on a set of gears to grip or release the bit. The difference is how the chuck is tightened. A keyed chuck (*inset drawing*) requires a chuck key to tighten the bit in place; a keyless chuck doesn't (*middle drawing*). There's no contest: Get a keyless chuck. You'll never miss searching around the shop for that missing key.

DRILL RECOMMENDATIONS

We all hate to hear it, but "How much are you willing to spend?" is a question you'll need to answer when buying a drill. What you need to be careful of is overbuying—buying more tool than you'll need (or be comfortable with). The common buying philosophy of "the more power, the better" doesn't always work. I have a friend who couldn't wait to buy the newest, most powerful drill. Unfortunately, it collects dust on his tool shelf because it's so heavy and bulky he can hardly lift it. For all-purpose work, I recommend a 9.6-volt or 12-volt cordless with a keyless chuck and two batteries. Then, for those jobs that require a more powerful drill, buy a heavy-duty ¹/₂" corded drill. Between these two drills, you can tackle almost any job.

DRILL PRESSES

There are three basic types of drill press to choose from: floor-model, bench-top, and a radial drill press.

Floor-model drill press

A floor-model drill press offers the largest work capacity of all the drill press types (*top photo*). You can safely drill into a workpiece as long as 48". (The work capacity of a drill press is the distance from the drill chuck to the base.) Although it's not likely that you'll need this capacity often, you'll be glad that you have it when you do need it.

Most drill presses have an adjustable table that can swing out of the way so you can rest a long work-piece directly on the base. This table slides up and down on a hollow steel column. The head of the drill press, which contains the motor, quill, and chuck, is mounted to the top of the column; the base mounts to the bottom (*bottom drawing*).

Bits are gripped in a three-jaw drill chuck, which spins inside a movable quill. Handles on the side of the head allow you to move the quill up and down. The amount of quill movement is referred to as its stroke and indicates how deep you can drill into a workpiece in a single pass.

Inside the drill head you'll typically find a set of stepped pulleys and one or two V-belts. By moving the V-belt(s) to various positions on the pulley(s), you can select different speeds. Some drill press manufacturers make a version with a continuously variable speed feature, but these can be quite costly.

Cover Conceals V-belt and Pulleys

Power Switch

Quill

Chuck

Table

Base

Motor

Feed Handle

Rack-and-Pinion System

Table-Height Adjustment Handle

Column

Bench-top drill press

Although some bench-top drill presses are light-duty, scaled-down versions of the floor-model drill presses, many aren't. As a matter of fact, you can find some that are more powerful and have better features than a floor-model (*top photo*). The major difference between a bench-top and a floor-model drill press is the work capacity—the distance between the base and the drill chuck. This is typically 16" on a bench-top drill press, and 44" to 48" on a floor model. Other than that, a quality bench-top drill press can do just about as much as a floor model.

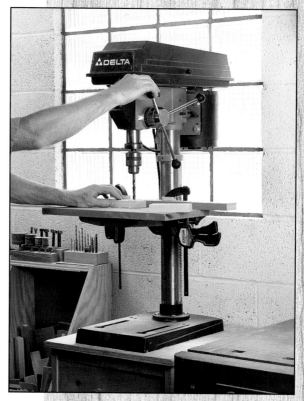

Radial drill press

Although a radial drill press has many of the same parts as a bench-top or floor-model drill press, a single glance will tell you it's a different breed of cat (*bottom photo*). A radial drill press is about the same size as the bench-top version, but with one huge difference: It has a much larger throat capacity (typically around 36"). That's because the head is attached to a horizontal ram column. This column is similar in size and function to the main column that supports the head. On some models the ram column moves in and out via a rack-and-pinion mechanism.

For angled drilling, the head and ram column can be rotated either to the left or to the right. Most models also allow you to pivot the head on the main column so that you can drill compound-angle holes easily. Sounds great, right? So why aren't radial drill presses more popular? A couple of reasons. First, with all the extra parts required and the additional manufacturing time, radial drill presses are more expensive than the other type—you can expect to pay around 50% more for a radial drill press. Second, radial drill presses have a reputation for not being as accurate as a standard drill press. A common complaint is that the bit tends to go out of square when throat capacity is adjusted.

DRILL PRESS FEATURES

Just like selecting a drill, choosing the right drill press is a matter of identifying the type of work you're planning on doing and then comparing the features of different models. For most of us, the feature that comes to mind immediately is the capacity of the drill press, in terms of both chuck-to-column and throat capacities (*see below*). But there are other features that are just as important. You'll also want to look closely at a couple of things. First, the table: its type, size, and ability to tilt. Second, the speeds available and the method of changing them.

Capacities

Drill presses are sized according to their throat capacity—the distance from the center of the chuck to the column (*top photo*). What can be confusing is that drill-press manufacturers double this when they advertise their products. For example, a drill press with a throat capacity of 6" is marketed as a "12" drill press" because it can drill to the center of a 12"-wide board. This is a case where bigger is better. Shown in the middle drawing are (1) throat capacity, (2) stroke, (3) length capacity, and (4) table size.

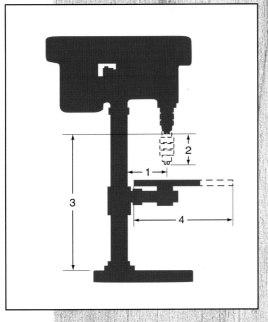

The type, size, and features of the table are also important. The main table types are round and square. Go with square/rectangular, as it's easier to clamp a workpiece to. As to size, pick the largest table you can afford, since it'll offer the most support for a workpiece. Finally, make sure the table tilts for drilling angled holes.

Speeds

Every drill press is capable of running at different speeds—typically between 20 and 3,600 rpm. Most use an induction motor that runs at a constant speed; to change speeds, you move a V-belt on stepped pulleys (*bottom photo*). Many bench-top models offer 5 speeds, while most floor models come with at least 12. The larger the selection, the easier it is to match the speed to the material you're drilling into.

Table tilt

You can drill angled holes on the drill press by tilting the table (*top photo*). It's worth the time to check out what you have to do to get it to tilt. On some models, you simply loosen a knob or handle, tilt the table, and tighten the knob. Other versions, like the one shown here, require you to remove a stop before the table can be tilted.

Table adjustment

The tables on all drill presses move up and down to adjust the position of the workpiece relative to the drill chuck. Many older models and some inexpensive modern models use a slip collar; basically, when a bolt or thumbscrew is loosened, the table is slid up or down. The disadvantage to this is the table is heavy and has to be supported when it's moved. A big improvement over a slip-collar table adjustment is an interlocking rack-and-pinion system; it supports the table at all times (*middle photo*). You can adjust it with one hand; just loosen the locking mechanism and turn the crank on the table to move it smoothly up or down. This type of table adjustment also makes it easy to fine-tune the position of the table—something that's quite difficult with a slip collar.

DRILL PRESS RECOMMENDATIONS

For all-around general use, I recommend a bench-top drill press with a minimum of five speeds and a ³/₄-hp induction motor. It'll handle almost any job, and you can use the space below it for storage. If you're working primarily in wood, look for a drill press with a slow speed (around 250 rpm)—many specialty bits work best at lower speeds. Make sure that the speeds are easy to change. If you know you'll be working on long or tall stock, a floor-model drill press will be a better choice.

When you've narrowed down your choices to just a few, keep a couple things in mind. First, stick with a name brand you can trust. Reputable tool manufacturers that have been around for decades are still in business for a reason: They make quality products. And, just as important, you can get replacement parts, even for their older machines. Second, a "bargain" tool usually isn't a bargain. It's cheaper because it was manufactured with looser tolerances and fewer steps. Take a look at the castings and the machined surfaces—they'll be clean and smooth on a quality drill press.

DRILL BITS

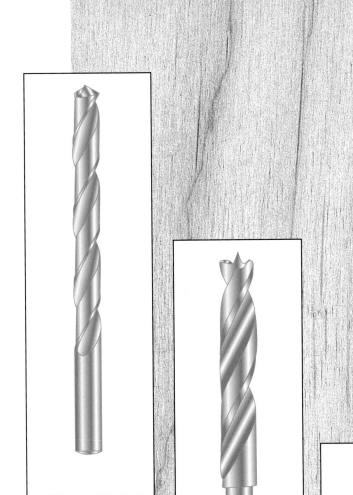

Twist bits

Twist bits can drill into just about anything because they're ground to a "universal" angle, usually 118 or 135 degrees (*top left drawing*). When buying bits, look for high-speed steel and a reputable manufacturer. Stay away from bargain bits; they may be inexpensive, but they won't last. Some manufacturers increase bit longevity with coatings. The most common is titanium-nitride (identifiable by the bright gold color), which increases resistance to wear and abrasion.

Brad-point bits

Brad-point bits excel at drilling round, clean holes in wood (*center drawing*). On a quality brad-point bit, the spurs protrude from the lips; this is the way a true brad-point bit is designed to work: The spurs score the wood, and the lips pare it away. On the bargain bits, the spurs and lips are ground in the same plane; they cut at the same time and there's no pre-scoring. The result is more tear-out and a ragged hole.

Spade bits

Although used primarily in construction trades for drilling holes in wood, a spade bit is just the ticket for many around-the-house jobs (*bottom right drawing*). How can you tell a good spade bit from a bad one? Look for spurs. Older spade bits have none. Newer ones have a set of cutting spurs on the outer corners of the blade. These spurs score the perimeter of the hole before the center is scraped away, resulting is a much cleaner hole.

Forstner bits

Forstner bits can handle problem drilling jobs like drilling clean holes at a steep angle, partial holes, and even overlapping holes. Instead of being guided by a centerpoint like other bits, a Forstner bit is guided by its rim (*top left drawing*). The rim scores the wood while a pair of lifters plane away the waste. The result is a clean, flat-bottomed hole. When shopping for these bits, look for a combination of high-speed steel and a small centerpoint.

Multi-spur bits

A popular derivation of the Forstner bit is the multi-spur bit. Unlike a Forstner bit, which uses a rim to score the perimeter of the cut, a multi-spur bit uses a set of jagged teeth (*far right drawing*). The gullets between the teeth efficiently whisk away chips. This means the bits can be run at higher speeds and will stand up to heat better. But multi-spur bits don't cut angled, partial, or overlapping holes as cleanly as a Forstner bit can.

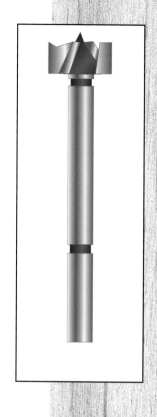

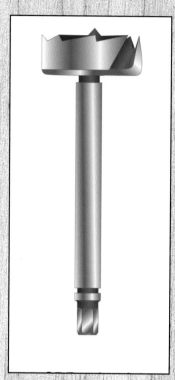

STOPPED HOLES

In woodworking and carpentry, it's often necessary to drill a "stopped" hole—one that doesn't go all the way through a workpiece, typically when a bolt or other piece of hardware needs to be recessed below the surface of the workpiece. Some bits are better for this task than others. It's easy to see why when you look at their profiles (*photo above left*).

The ultimate bit for the job is a Forstner bit because it leaves a flat-bottomed hole and has a small centerpoint; the flatter the hole, the better it can support a washer and distribute weight more evenly when a bolt or screw is tightened. Brad-point and twist bits are the second best choice—they too have small centerpoints and produce a relatively flat bottom. A spade bit, with its large centerpoint, should be used only if the workpiece is thick or if the bit is to break through the other side.

SPECIALTY BITS

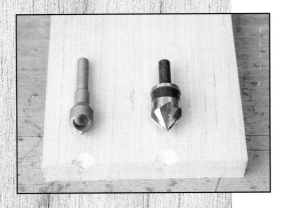

Countersink bits

Typically used after a shank hole is drilled, a countersink bit creates a depression in the material to fit the head of the screw (*top photo*). There are two types of countersink bits: The most common has a series of flutes to scrape the depression (often producing a scalloped cut); the other type has a single cutting edge that slices the wood and leaves a much cleaner hole.

Pilot bits

A pilot bit makes installing screws painless because it drills the pilot hole, shank hole, countersink, and (if desired) a counterbore all at the same time (*middle photo*). Screw pilot bits allow you to adjust the length of the pilot hole but don't let you adjust the length of the shank hole. Taper pilot bits offer a separate countersink and stop collar that slide up and down on a bit tapered to match the profile of a standard wood screw.

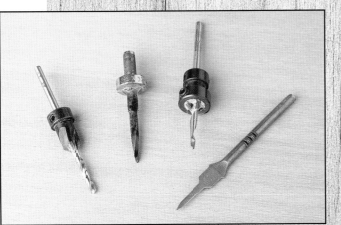

VIX BITS

A self-centering (or Vix) bit is a totally reliable way to install a hinge or other piece of hardware without the usual skewing and misalignment (*photo at right*). The "magic" of this bit is an inner and outer sleeve that spin around a twist bit (*drawing at right*). When the tip of the self-centering bit is inserted in a hinge hole and depressed, an inner sleeve retracts up into the outer sleeve. This positions the twist bit so it can drill a perfectly centered hole for the hinge screw.

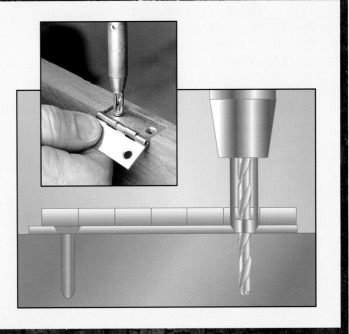

Hole saws

When you need to drill holes greater than $1^1/2$" in diameter, reach for a hole saw (*top photo*). The most common type consists of two parts: a twist bit that guides the cut, and a metal cup with saw teeth that do the cutting. The cup is usually carbon steel or bimetal. Regardless of the type, it's essential that you use slow speeds and stop often to blow out sawdust that can build up and cause burning.

Drum and disk sanders

A drum sander is a rubber cylinder with an arbor running through it that, when tightened, expands to grip a sanding sleeve. Drum sander sizes vary from $1/2$" $\times$ $1/2$" up to 3" $\times$ 3". They can be mounted in a drill press (*middle photo*) or used in a portable drill. When shopping for these, pay extra for a longer set; not only do these allow you to sand thicker materials, but also the larger sanding surface helps your sanding sleeves last longer, since you can distribute wear and tear over the entire length of the sanding sleeve.

A disk sander is just a rubber disk (with an arbor) that accepts pressure-sensitive adhesive (PSA) sandpaper (*middle inset photo*). All disks are not the same. A thin rubber disk is very flexible—great if you're sanding a curved surface; but if you're working on a flat surface, a rigid disk is better.

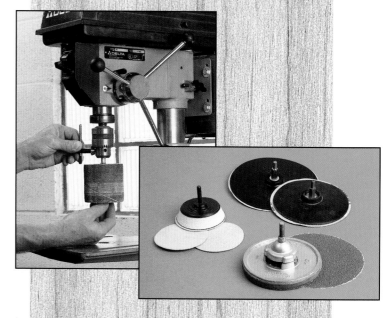

Wire wheels and buffing pads

A wire wheel fitted with an arbor or a wire brush can quickly remove rust and old paint from metal (*bottom photo*). Wire wheels are usually 5" in diameter and usually come in two "grits"—fine and coarse. Buffing wheels combined with a little jeweler's rouge will rapidly bring a high luster to metal tools, jewelry, etc. Usually made of muslin, buffing wheels come in 3", 4", and 6" diameters. Buffing pads (or bonnets) are designed to slip over a rubber disk (*bottom inset photo*). You'll find them in diameters ranging from 5" to 10".

SPEED SELECTION

The type of material that you're drilling into will affect the drill speed, the feed rate (the amount of pressure you apply to the drill), and the type of lubricant, if any, you use. As a general rule of thumb, the harder the material, the lower the drill speed (*see the drill speed chart below left*).

In terms of size, the smaller the bit, the greater the speed needed for effective cutting. Conversely, as the bit gets larger, your speed should decrease. But there's more to drilling a hole than selecting the correct speed. The feed rate (pressure you apply to the drill) is also important. But what may not seem obvious is that feed rate directly affects the bit's cutting speed.

Let's say, for instance, you're drilling into softwood with a $1/4$" twist bit at a recommended speed of 1,000 rpm. If you were to drill five holes, varying the feed rate from 1" to 5" per second, you'd get cleaner holes at the lower feed rates. Why? Because although the bit speed is constant, you're changing how quickly the bit cuts into the wood. In effect, you're increasing the bit speed away from its recommended speed.

Although this can get confusing, there's a really simple way to determine both correct speed and feed rate: Just listen to the motor as you drill. The sound that the motor makes is your best indication of proper combination of speed and feed rate. Start with the recommended speed for the material for the size hole you're drilling. As you begin to drill, listen. If the motor begins to bog down, back off on the feed rate. If it sounds like it's free-running and not really cutting into the material, increase the feed rate. It's just like listening to your lawnmower as you mow the lawn. If you go too fast, it bogs down; too slow, and you're not cutting effectively. With a little practice, you'll quickly learn the "right" sound that your drill makes when it's drilling at the correct combination of speed and feed rate.

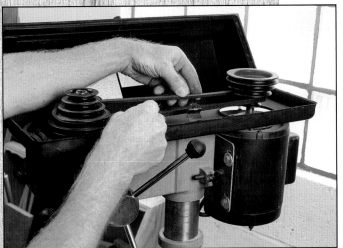

SPEEDS/MATERIALS

Material	Speed (in rpm)
Softwoods	800–2,400
Hardwoods	600–1,800
Ferrous metals	100–900
Nonferrous metals	300–2,400
Masonry	100–800
Glass	300–2,400
Plastics	300–1,400

DRILLING IN WOOD

For the most part, drilling into wood is simplicity itself. No lubricant is necessary, and the speed and feed rate will be determined by the type (and species) of wood you're drilling into, such as hardwood, softwood, plywood, or other manmade composite products.

Shavings

In addition to the sound the drill motor makes, there's another quick indication that you've hit the right combination of drill speed and feed rate: the wood shavings themselves (*top photo*). If they're uniform in size and the bit isn't clogging, you've selected an appropriate speed/feed rate combination. If you're not getting nice curly shavings (and you're sure that your bit is sharp), continue searching for the right speed/feed rate combination.

Backer boards

The big challenge to drilling wood is preventing tear-out. Tear-out occurs when a bit breaks through the opposite side and the fibers of the wood are unsupported. A dependable way to prevent this is to back up the workpiece with some scrap wood (*middle drawing*). Since the workpiece is supported by the scrap, no tear-out occurs. It's also wise to use a backer board whenever you're drilling through a workpiece on the drill press. The only thing to be careful of is to make sure the center hole in the drill press table is centered roughly underneath your bit. This way if you accidentally drill through the backer board, you won't ruin the bit by hitting a metal table.

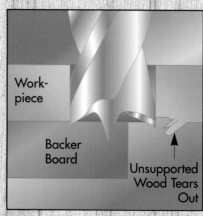

Work-piece

Backer Board

Unsupported Wood Tears Out

DRILLING IN BOTH DIRECTIONS

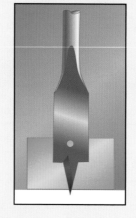

▨ Another way to prevent tear-out is to drill from both directions. This is a particularly useful tip when using drill bits with a long centerpoint (such as a spade bit). To do this, drill into the workpiece until the point just begins to break through the opposite side (*above drawing*). Then use this indent to start your drill bit from the opposite direction (*drawing above right*). With this method, if any tear-out does occur, it happens inside the hole and will not be seen.

DRILLING IN METAL

Drilling in metal is simple as long as you follow a few basic rules. First, make sure you use a sharp bit. You can get away with drilling into wood with a not-so-sharp bit, but not metal—it just doesn't work. Second, always centerpunch to prevent the bit from wandering. Third, use slow speeds and the proper lubricant. As a general rule of thumb, the softer the material, the higher the speed to cut effectively.

The type of lubricant you use will depend on what you're drilling (*see the chart below left*). Lubricants keep the bit cool by reducing heat-generating friction, which can damage both your bits and your workpiece. A lubricant also helps to keep the hole clean by floating away small metal particles and shavings that can clog up a twist drill. Don't get carried away with lubricant, though. A small puddle the size of a penny will do in most cases; any more and you'll end up with a shirt or shop apron that looks like you've been hanging around the spin art booth at the local fair.

Securing the workpiece

There are a couple of really good reasons you should always clamp a metal workpiece to the table of the drill press before drilling (*top photo*). First, drilling creates friction, and the resulting heat can quickly make the workpiece too hot to handle. Second, twist drills have a tendency to "catch" the material as they exit, and spin the workpiece—even throw it.

A lubricant well

Lubricants can't do their job if they don't stay where they're needed—at the cutting edge of the bit. To keep lubricants (especially thin ones) where they can do some good, make a small well or "moat" around the bit (*middle photo*). Plumber's putty works great for this. Roll some into a coil and wrap it around the bit, leaving about $1/2$" between the putty and the bit. Pour in a small amount of lubricant, and drill.

LUBRICANTS

Material	Lubricant
Wood	None
Hard Steel	Turpentine
Machine Steel	Soluble Oil
Wrought Iron	Lard Oil
Brass	Kerosene
Glass	Kerosene
Aluminum	Kerosene
Plastic	None

DRILLING IN PLASTIC

Just as with wood, drilling into plastic is simple (*top photo*). No lubricant is necessary, and the speed and feed rate will depend on the material you're drilling into. The trickiest part to drilling plastic is finding the correct speed/feed rate combination.

Although you won't experience tear-out in plastic as you do in wood, it is quite possible for an exiting bit to break or chip off small pieces of plastic. This is often the case when you're drilling into plastic laminates (such as Formica). The thin layers of these are prone to chipping. To prevent this, you can use the same measures used for wood: Support the work with a scrap piece, or drill from both sides.

Because plastic will melt when sufficient heat is present, it's important to keep both the workpiece and drill bit cool. The simplest way to do this is to frequently lift the bit out as you drill to clear out friction- and heat-generating chips. This is particularly important if you're drilling into thermosetting plastic.

If you're drilling holes to accept metal hardware (screws, nails, and so forth), it's best to drill the holes slightly oversized (around $1/64$" to $1/32$"). This allows for the inevitable expansion and contraction of the plastic. Also, if you plan to work with plastic often, consider purchasing a set of bits designed for drilling in plastic. Although they're similar in appearance to twist bits, the tips of these are ground to a sharper angle, typically around 60 degrees.

Shavings

When you drill into plastic, the shavings should peel off in tightly coiled corkscrews (*bottom photo*). If you go too fast, the plastic may chip, crack, or shatter. Too slow and heat may build up, resulting in a nifty melted plastic blob with your bit stuck in it. I'd recommend drilling a couple of test holes in a piece of similar scrap plastic before drilling into your workpiece.

DRIVING SCREWS

One of the most labor-saving applications of an electric drill is its ability to drive screws (*top photo*). A cordless drill with a clutch and a hefty battery—a driver/drill—is the best tool for driving screws. A corded drill, however, may be a wiser choice for a lengthy job where you'll need a lot of torque (such as driving long deck screws into pressure-treated lumber when building a deck or gazebo).

Pilot holes

Regardless of the type of drill you're using to drive screws, it's often a good idea to first drill a pilot hole (*middle photo*). Drilling a pilot hole effectively reduces the impact of material density by removing it instead of trying to displace it with the screw. This is basically an all-around good idea whenever you drive screws into wood—especially near the end of a board, where it's prone to splitting.

Clutch

If your drill has a clutch, driving screws is just a matter of finding the appropriate setting and then driving the screw flush (*bottom photo*). But getting used to clutch settings and finding the right one for the job will take some experimentation. The greater the number of settings, the better your chance of finding the perfect one. With a bit of practice, you'll be able to get within a setting or two on the first try. If you're lucky enough to be working on a project with consistent materials (like attaching drywall to metal studs), you'll be able to set the clutch and drive screws with perfect regularity. However, when you're working with a more finicky material (such as hardwood or softwood), the variations can cause you to spin the clutch settings like a frantic teenager who has forgotten the combination to a school locker.

PORTABLE-DRILL PRECISION

Portable drills aren't known for their precision. Granted, there are plenty of jobs where you don't need to be super-precise—you're drilling into drywall to install plastic anchors, or drilling pilot holes in decking for screws. But there are those times when accuracy counts. Sure, the size of the hole you're drilling will be accurate—the right-sized drill bit will take care of that. But drilling perfectly straight holes can be a challenge.

Fortunately, no matter what type of material you're drilling into, there are a number of ways you can increase the accuracy and precision of your portable drill. To drill to a specific depth, you can buy commercially made stops, or you can use a simple shop-made version (*see below*). If you need to make sure the hole you're drilling is straight, there are a number of sight guides, drilling guides, and levels that you can buy or make that will make this easy.

Depth stops

The most common manufactured depth stop is a metal collar that slips over the bit. A small setscrew locks the collar in place. The disadvantage to this is that tightening the setscrew can crush the bit's flutes, resulting in poor chip ejection and clogging. I've always gotten along with two simple shop-made versions that don't harm the bit: a piece of masking tape wrapped around a bit (*top photo*), and a scrap block of wood with a hole in it (*middle photo*).

Sight guides

Perhaps the simplest method for drilling an accurate straight or angled hole is to use one of your layout tools as a reference. For straight holes, set a small try square or combination square alongside your drill bit and use it as a guide for your drill (*bottom photo*). Even a block of wood that's cut reliably square will work in a pinch as a simple sight reference.

Bubble levels

An alternative to a sight guide is a bubble level. Bubble levels come built-in on some drills and are available as "stick-on" accessories for those that don't. These are an invaluable aid when drilling in tight or awkward quarters, where it isn't feasible to use a sight guide. To use a bubble level, just position the drill so the bubble indicates you're level, and then drill away (*top photo*).

Pilot holes

Even if you use a guide or level, you're out of luck if the bit wanders off your mark. Assuming you have marked and center-punched your hole, it's still a common problem for a bit to wander, especially if you're using a twist bit (although true flat-bottomed Forstner bits are also tough to start). Fortunately, the fix is easy. Just start by drilling a small pilot hole all the way through for your larger bit to "follow" (*middle photo*).

Drilling guides

The next step up in accuracy from a sight guide is a drilling guide. The concept is simple. Precision holes are drilled in a guide block to support the bit along its length (*bottom photo*). As you drill, this support prevents you from tilting the bit, ensuring the correct angle. You can purchase manufactured drilling guides, but you can also use a simple shop-made guide block that will work just as effectively.

DRILL PRESS PRECISION

Unlike a portable drill, precision is what a drill press is all about. Whether you need a perfectly straight hole, or to drill to an exact depth, the drill press is the tool for the job. But like all mechanical marvels, a drill press needs to be tuned and adjusted in order to guarantee a high level of precision. Fortunately, this takes only a couple minutes and should be done whenever precision is paramount or anytime you adjust the table; *see below.*

There are also a number of simple tricks that you can do to make your drill press even more precise. In particular, add clamping tools, fences, and stops to your drill press table so you can quickly and accurately position a workpiece. These tricks are especially useful for repetitive work like drilling holes in identical parts.

Align table

Aligning a drill press table so that it's perfectly perpendicular to the drill chuck is a snap with this quick and easy procedure. Chuck a 5" or 6" length of straight $1/2$" metal rod in the drill. Then butt a small try square up against the rod. Loosen the table-tilt nut or bolt, adjust the table until there's no gap between the blade of the try square and the rod, and tighten (*top photo*).

Check quill

If you notice that the centerpoints on your bits tend to wobble slightly when in the drill press, first roll them on a known-flat surface to make sure they're not bent. If they're straight, the quill may need some attention. You can check the quill for "runout" by using a dial indicator as shown in the bottom photo (*see page 76 for more on this procedure*).

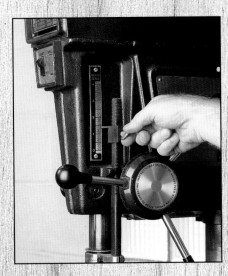

Depth stop

Drilling a hole to an exact depth is child's play for a drill press. Position the workpiece next to the bit, and lower the quill to the desired depth marked on the workpiece. Then adjust the depth-stop nut or the rotating depth scale to lock the quill in this position (*top photo*). Drill a test hole in a scrap piece and check the depth. Adjust as necessary.

Spindle lock

You can accurately lock the quill in any position along its stroke with the quill lock (*middle photo*). This is most often done when using a drum sander or other abrasive tool on the drill press.

Repetitive work

When you need to drill an accurate series of holes in similar-shaped parts (like a set of wheel axles for a toy train), consider this quick setup. First, position the workpiece on the drill press table, aligning it to the bit. Then set a framing square or a try square against two adjacent sides of the part and clamp the square directly to the drill press table (*bottom photo*). This forms a dual fence to quickly position each part for drilling.

Fence

One of the best ways to accurately position a workpiece for drilling is to use a fence. This can be as simple as a 2×4, or as fancy as the commercial fences available from mail-order catalogs. In either case, place the workpiece on the table so the bit is roughly aligned with the mark on the workpiece. Then position the fence so the bit and mark are perfectly aligned, and clamp it in place. Horizontal stops take a fence to a higher level of precision. A horizontal stop is just a scrap of wood clamped to the fence. It "stops" a workpiece from sliding from side to side when a hole is bored.

MORTISING ATTACHMENT

A mortising attachment for a drill press can make the tedious job of cutting mortises for joinery quick and accurate. But drilling mortises still takes time. Granted, the mortising drill quickly removes the majority of the wood, but the chisel that shears the sides square uses good old-fashioned elbow grease—supplied by you.

The key to successful mortising is the setup of the attachment. There's nothing complicated about it; you just have to take your time to adjust everything properly. A few things to note. First, disconnect the power to the drill press before beginning work. Second, make sure to read and follow the manufacturer's directions thoroughly. Third, whenever possible, buy a mortising attachment made by the manufacturer of your drill press. You can often fit another brand on your drill, but not without some fiddling.

Setup

The first step is to attach the chisel holder to the drill press (*top photo*). In most cases, the holder attaches to the quill. Lower the quill a couple of inches and lock it in place. Depending on your mortising attachment, you may need to insert rubber rings between the quill and the holder. Most attachments come with an alignment pin to help position the holder.

Adjust bit

Once the holder is in place, you can install the mortising chisel and bit (*middle photo*). Insert the chisel in the holder so the chip-ejection slots are facing the left or right of the drill press (this provides the best ejection and prevents heat buildup). Then slide the mortising bit up into the chisel so that the upper face of the chisel is approximately $1/32$" below the bottom edge of the holder, and tighten the thumbscrew.

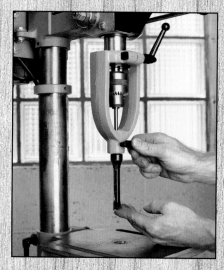

MORTISING BITS

The secret to "drilling" square holes with a mortising attachment is the bits. An auger-type bit rotates within a square-edged hollow chisel (*photo at left*). The bit cuts a round hole, and the chisel punches the corners square. Both parts must be very sharp for this to work. The chisels come in a variety of sizes; the most common are $1/4$", $5/16$", $3/8$", $1/2$", and $3/4$".

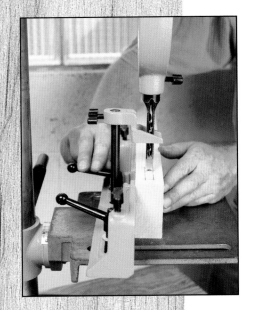

Align fence

Attach the fence to the drill press table with the mounting hardware supplied (*top photo*). Then loosen the locking levers and shift the fence to bring the workpiece into the desired position under the mortising chisel. Then slide the workpiece along the fence to make sure the mortise will be cut along the desired line. Attach the vertical hold-down to the fence, and adjust it to press the workpiece firmly against the table with light pressure.

Depth stop

Place the workpiece against the fence and raise the drill press table until the chisel clears the top edge of the workpiece by about 1/2". Then lower the quill to the desired depth and lock the depth stop in position (*middle photo*). For mortises that will be cut through the entire width or thickness of the stock, make sure to insert a scrap block under the workpiece before making the depth adjustments.

Cut mortises

Before you cut into any actual workpieces, take the time first to make a test cut in a scrap block. Double-check the mortise location and depth. Then to cut a full mortise, start by making the extreme or end cuts (*bottom photo*). Then take a series of overlapping cuts to remove the waste between the ends. Raise the quill often to aid in chip ejection. Patience will be rewarded here—forcing the chisel would only generate heat, which would cause the wood to burn and the bit to dull.

DRILL PRESS QUILL

As I've mentioned previously, a drill press is supposed to drill accurate and precise holes. In order for this to happen, the quill must be true and the chuck mounted perfectly straight on the spindle. If either one of these is out of alignment—a condition referred to as runout—the bit will wobble, and starting a hole at a precise point will be almost impossible. You can check for runout with a dial indicator, or use an inexpensive low-tech version using a block of wood and a feeler gauge.

Dial indicator

The most reliable and accurate way to check your quill for runout is to use a dial indicator (*see the sidebar below*). Unplug the drill press; then butt the indicator probe up against the chuck (*top photo*). Turn the motor pulley or belt by hand to rotate the chuck. Movement in excess of 0.005" indicates excessive runout.

Feeler gauge

If you don't have a dial indicator, you can still check for runout with this low-tech method. Unplug the drill press and insert a large-diameter bit. Raise the table up so about 1" of the shank is exposed. Then press a scrap of wood against the shank. Rotate the motor pulley or belt by hand. Any runout will force the block away from the shank. Measure the largest gap with a feeler gauge; here again, 0.005" is excessive (*middle photo*).

DIAL INDICATOR

My favorite tool for checking for runout is a dial indicator like the one shown in the photo at left. It's fitted with a magnetic base that holds it securely to your drill press table bed. You can take measurements in increments of one thousandth of an inch.

Test for excessive play

In addition to a bent spindle, excessive runout can be caused by worn-out bearings. To check for this, first lower the quill as far as it will go and lock it in place with the quill lock. Then grip the quill, as shown, and try to move it from side to side (*top photo*). If the bearings are OK, there should be no movement at all. If you can shift the quill, the bearings need to be replaced—a service center is your best bet.

Adjust for runout

An improperly seated drill chuck is often the cause of runout. To correct the problem, tighten a large-diameter drill bit in the chuck. Strike the shank of the bit with a hammer on the side that runs out—that is, the side that caused the scrap block or dial indicator to move the most (*middle photo*). After you've adjusted the chuck, check the runout again, and repeat as necessary. If the runout is still excessive, the spindle is likely bent and needs to be replaced.

Alignment marks

If a drilling job requires absolute precision, you can check for and adjust for runout with the bit you're planning on using. If you're likely to repeat the job in the future—say, for instance, you're reboring the arbor hole on saw blades—you can save the setup time by making a set of scribe marks on both the chuck and the drill bit (*bottom photo*). Then the next time you need to drill with this bit, all you have to do is align the marks for rock-solid precision.

"A power plane can do in a few minutes what might require a day or more by hand. In a creative craft, it becomes a question of responsibility, whether it is man or the machine that controls the works progress."

GEORGE NAKASHIMA (1981)

JOINTERS and PLANERS

In a perfect square, the sides are perpendicular to the faces. In a perfect world, the stock you buy is square. In woodworking, results absolutely depend on square stock. The problem? No matter where you buy your wood, it won't be square. Period. How do you solve this dilemma? With the jointer and the planer.

In just moments, as Mr. Nakashima says, a power planer can accomplish a day's handwork. And those moments will dictate the outcome of a project, because the only way stock gets square is if you make it so. And the tools you'll use to do this are the jointer and the planer. Along with the tablesaw, they make up the "power triangle" that's a must for any shop.

We've all bought off-the-shelf lumber that's labeled "surfaced four sides." This doesn't mean it's square. Wood is an organic material, moving constantly to react to changes in its environment. Even "air-dried" lumber sitting outside in a lumberyard isn't dry: Once you bring it home, it takes weeks to stop losing moisture and stop moving so you can start to work with it.

In our imperfect world, the jointer and planer are perfectly invaluable.

The rugged old portable power planer shown here still works great. It's a Craftsman industrial power planer, model number 315.25020. Its 2" spiral blade is relatively narrow compared to modern planers (typically 4" or wider), but it handled the job it was designed for—planing doors and trim to size.

Types of Jointers

A jointer consists of two parallel tables with a spinning cutterhead in the middle that shaves off small amounts of wood from a workpiece that's passed over it (*top drawing*). Stock is fed into the cutterhead via the infeed table, and the outfeed table supports the freshly jointed workpiece. The knives of the cutterhead and the outfeed table are set to the same height. The infeed table on all jointers slides up and down to control the depth of cut. There are two basic types of jointers: bench-top and stationary.

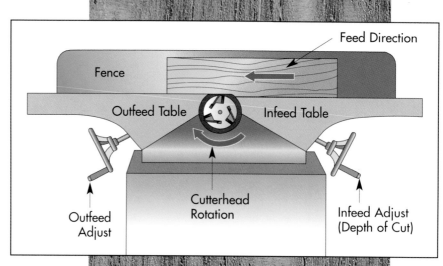

Feed Direction

Fence

Outfeed Table   Infeed Table

Cutterhead Rotation

Outfeed Adjust

Cutterhead Rotation

Infeed Adjust (Depth of Cut)

Bench-top

Bench-top jointers have limited use in the shop because they have a short bed and an underpowered motor (*middle photo*). They do, however, work fine for short stock on limited runs. I know a number of woodcrafters who find this type of jointer adequate for their needs—and its diminutive size makes it easier to shoehorn it into a small space. Although these small jointers often have a reasonably wide bed (6"), their small universal motor just doesn't have the power to handle the job. The advantage of a universal motor, though, is that you can vary the speed. The other advantage to a bench-top jointer is its price: Most sell for well under $300.

Stationary

A stationary jointer is a better choice for the average woodworker, as the bed length is better matched to the table width (*bottom photo*). Stationary jointers range in size from 6" up to a whopping 16". Many woodworkers find a 6" jointer will do the job; but if funds and space permit, an 8" jointer is a better choice. As the bed widens, the tables lengthen. And the longer the tables, the more accurate and easy it is to flatten lumber. Prices range from $400 to $1,200 for 6" jointers and $600 to $2,300 for the larger units.

JOINTER FEATURES

Bed width and length

The width of a jointer's bed determines the maximum cut (*top photo*). Most wood-workers opt for a 6" jointer because of cost, but end up wishing they'd purchased an 8" model. The extra 2" makes a big difference when preparing rough stock—you'll often encounter boards that are wider than 6". With a 6" jointer, you'll need to rip the board before you can surface it. With short beds, it's all too easy to end up with a bowed board because the ends of the board aren't in constant contact with the bed. A long bed fully supports the stock, creating an accurate reference to make a straight cut.

Motor size and type

The two types of motors you'll find on joint-ers are universal and induction. Bench-top joint-ers utilize universal motors and can tackle only small jobs. Stationary jointers feature heavy-duty induction motors designed for heavier loads. They spin the cutterhead via a belt (*middle photo*). The higher the horsepower and amperage rating, the stronger the motor. Note that most 8" and larger jointers require 220 volts to run. This is another reason many woodworkers end up with a smaller 6" jointer—they run off 110 volts.

Infeed/outfeed adjustment

Since the infeed adjustment is the main adjustment for a jointer, it's important that the adjustment mechanism be both easy to use and accessible. My preference is for a hand wheel (like the one shown in the bottom photo), but some woodworkers prefer the lever style common on some models. Regardless of the handle or lever, make sure that there's a positive locking mechanism that will prevent the table from shifting out of position in use. Whenever possible, select a jointer where both the infeed and the outfeed tables are adjustable.

Knife changing

To be honest, changing knives on a jointer is a hassle. That's why it's important to check out any jointer you're interested in to see what the procedure is for changing knives. One feature that's nice is a cutter-head lock; see the red metal bracket that flips up to lock the cutterhead in place in the photo *at right*. This prevents the cutter-head from rotating out of position as you adjust the knives. Also look to see whether the gibs (the metal bars that clamp the knives in place on the cutterhead) are secured with bolts or screws. I've found that Allen-head screws are often easier to adjust than bolts.

Fence

The fence on a jointer is one half of the critical equation that creates perpendicular adjacent edges. The fence on a quality jointer should be easy to adjust back and forth across the bed, as well as having a positive locking mechanism (*middle photo*). It should also feature linkages that allow you to tilt it when making angled cuts. Looks for built-in adjustable stops that set the fence at 90 and 45 degrees. Here again, make sure the locking system is positive and easy to use.

JOINTER RECOMMENDATIONS

Choosing a jointer is a fairly simple process. Start by identifying the type of work you do. If you work primarily with short stock and won't be working the machine very hard, a bench-top jointer will do the job. For the more serious wood-worker who is working with longer and wider stock, you'll want to purchase a sta-tionary jointer—either a 6" or an 8" model. If you've got the room in the shop, I heartily recommend buying an 8" jointer if you can afford it. I realize they're quite a bit more expensive, but I can't tell you how many woodworkers I know who pur-chased a 6" jointer and then realized they should have bought the larger 8" version. I also recommend buying or making a closed base. Enclosing the jointer base is the easiest way to capture and convey dust and chips away to a dust collector. This also keeps the motor, bearings, and belt cleaner, so they'll run smoother and longer.

JOINTER ACCESSORIES

Jointer push blocks

In addition to the pivoting guard that comes standard on every jointer, a push block is the next most important safety device (*top photo*). Some savvy manufacturers are now including a set with every jointer—that's because they know all too well how dangerous an exposed cutterhead can be. It's just a lot safer to run a board over a cutterhead with a safety barrier (the push block) between your hand and the workpiece. Let's face it—accidents do happen in the shop. One way to prevent a nasty one with a jointer is to use a push block whenever possible.

Knives

Virtually every jointer comes with a set of HSS (high-speed steel) knives (*middle photo*). These knives perform admirably in most shop situations, can be resharpened, and will last for years. If you need to purchase replacement knives, it's best to buy them from the original manufacturer to ensure they're the correct size and type. Note: For a longer-lasting edge, you might want to consider a set of carbide-tipped knives. This type of knife is a HSS body with a length of carbide permanently bonded to the tip. Carbide-tipped knives typically run 20% to 40% more than the HSS knives. Although they do hold an edge longer, they nick more easily and are much more costly to have sharpened.

Knife-setting jigs

Since changing jointer knives is a hassle, accessory manufacturers have come up with jigs to make the job easier. The most common is a magnetic knife-setting jig (*bottom photo*). This style of jig uses powerful magnets: one set to attach to the jointer bed, another set to hold the knives in position so that you can tighten the gib bolts. Most of these will work on jointers with knives up to 8" in width, regardless of the diameter of the cutterhead.

JOINTER: EDGE-JOINTING

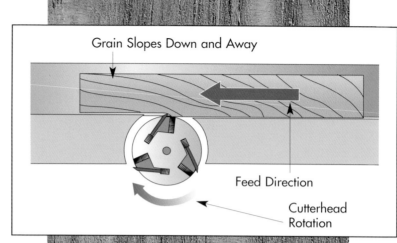

Grain Slopes Down and Away

Feed Direction

Cutterhead Rotation

Grain direction

Regardless of the type of jointing operation (face or edge), to get the smoothest cut you need to take into account the grain direction of the workpiece. For the best overall cut, the grain should slope down and away from the cutterhead, as shown in the drawing *at right*. In a perfect world, this is always possible. But any woodworker knows that grain can (and will) switch direction in a piece—often multiple times. In cases like this, try to joint the piece so the majority of the grain is sloping down and away—and take a very light cut.

Start the cut

Edge-jointing is a fairly straightforward operation, as long as you follow a couple of simple rules. First, make sure to press the face of the workpiece firmly into the side of the fence at all times in order to achieve a perpendicular cut (*middle photo*) on the edges. Second, position the workpiece a few inches away from the edge of the cutterhead so that it engages the guard, and then slowly feed the workpiece over the cutterhead. As the workpiece crosses the cutterhead, shift your weight to the outfeed table.

Finish the cut

It's a common misconception of many woodworkers that you should press down heavily on the infeed table. Although you should press down some here, the bulk of the pressure should always be on the outfeed table since this is your reference edge (*bottom photo*). That's why it's important to always shift your weight (and the pressure) to the outfeed side as soon as the workpiece passes the cutterhead.

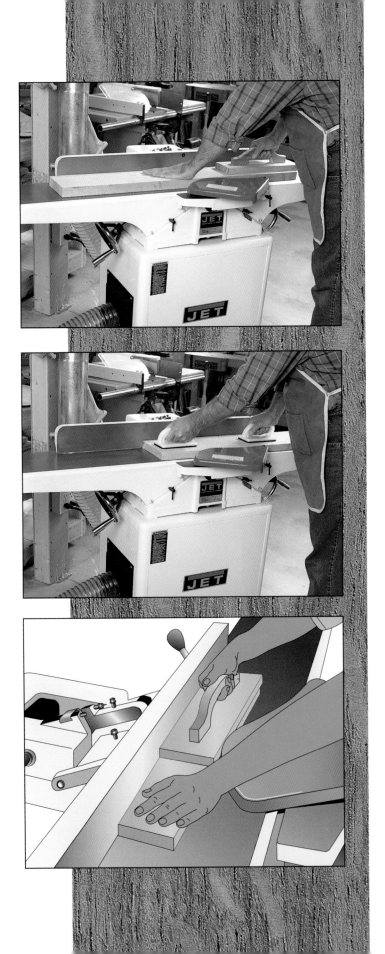

JOINTER: FACE-JOINTING

Push block

Every jointer manufacturer out there will tell you that the number one rule for face-jointing is: Never pass your hand directly over the cutterhead. That is, don't assume that the workpiece will protect you from the spinning knives. Workpieces (especially thin ones) can snap apart, allowing your hand to come in contact with the knives. The problem is that you need to apply downward pressure to the workpiece as it passes over the cutterhead. The solution is to use some form of push block. The lipped push block shown in the top photo works well for pushing the workpiece ahead, but it doesn't do much for downward pressure.

Grout float

A popular style of push block (that resembles a grout float) works extremely well for applying pressure to the workpiece as it passes over the cutterhead (*middle photo*). This is important for getting an even cut and prevents the workpiece from chattering (bouncing as it comes in contact with the cutterhead) and producing a ribbed cut. The disadvantage to grout float–style push blocks is that since they don't have a lip on the end to catch the workpiece, they have a tendency to slip during the cut.

Technique

Here's how I suggest face-jointing stock. Use a lipped push block to guide the workpiece into the cutterhead. If you have a grout float–style push block, set it directly over the end of the workpiece and apply downward pressure as it engages the cutterhead. Allow the workpiece to slide under the grout float–style push block as you continue to apply pressure just past the cutterhead directly over the outfeed table. If you're using hand pressure, allow the first 6" of the workpiece to pass the cutterhead before applying downward pressure (*bottom drawing*).

Specialty Jointer Cuts

End grain

Even though most woodworkers would never consider jointing end grain, it's quite doable as long as your knives are sharp and you take a light cut. The only worry is chip-out as you complete the cut. There are two methods to prevent this. The first method is to clamp a sacrificial scrap piece to the end of the work-piece and joint as usual (*top drawing*). The other method is a little trickier: Start jointing the end grain and then stop after about 2" to 3". Then flip the workpiece end for end and finish the cut. Be careful not to go past the previously jointed end grain, or it may chip out.

Plywood

Jointing plywood is another one of those procedures that make most woodworkers shudder. But here again, it's quite easy to do as long as you take light cuts and your knives are sharp (*middle drawing*). Why would you want to joint plywood? I've often done it on the edges of shelves on which I was planning to glue a strip to conceal the edge. The cleaner the edge, the better the glue joint. One thing to keep in mind: Since plywood contains a high glue content, which can act as an abrasive, dulling knives, use this technique sparingly.

Veneer

A final specialty cut that is a real problem solver is jointing the edges of veneer or laminate in order to get a perfect glue joint. To do this, just sandwich the pieces of veneer or laminate to be joined between two layers of plywood or other straight stock (*bottom drawing*). Position the veneer or laminate so it barely sticks out along its entire length. Then take a series of light cuts until you've exposed fresh wood along the full length of the veneer and the clamp blocks.

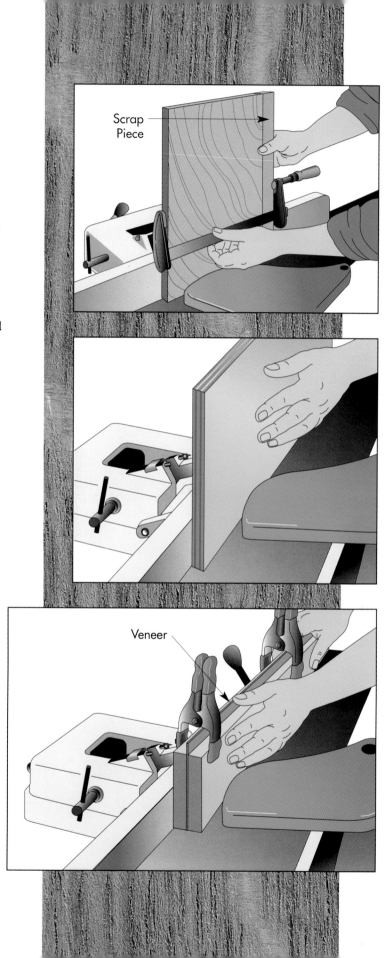

JOINTER: REMOVING CUP

One of the most common mistakes I've seen woodworkers make in the shop is trying to flatten cupped or warped stock with a planer. Granted, you will get a thicknessed board with parallel faces—the problem is, the cup or warp will most likely still be there. The reason for this is that the infeed and outfeed rollers of the planer are typically strong enough to hold the board flat as it passes under the cutterhead (*see page 92 for more on this*). But as soon as the board is free from this pressure, it'll spring back to its original form.

The way to get around this is to remove the cup or warp on one face with the jointer and then place the flattened face on the bed of the planer to serve as a reference for the other face. This method creates smooth, flat boards without cup or warp. (For more on the correct sequence for squaring stock, *see pages 96–97.*)

Flatten one face

The first step in removing cup is to place the board on the jointer with the concave face down, as shown in the top drawing *at left*. Set the jointer for a light cut (around 1/16") and, using push blocks, pass the board slowly over the cutterhead. Don't worry about keeping the edge of the board perfectly flush with the fence—you can joint a perpendicular edge after you've jointed the face flat. Take as many light passes as necessary until the face is flat. Tip: Scribble a pencil mark across the face of the board—when it's completely gone, the face is flat.

Flatten the other face

If possible, the preferred method for getting a parallel flat face is to run the board through a planer once one face is flat. If you don't have access to one, you can get a fairly parallel face with the jointer alone. Start by jointing one edge perpendicular to the flattened face. Then position the workpiece with the concave face down and with the jointed edge against the fence (*bottom drawing*). The key thing here is to keep the jointed edge butted firmly against the fence to prevent the board from rocking or tipping as you cut. Take light cuts and go slowly here.

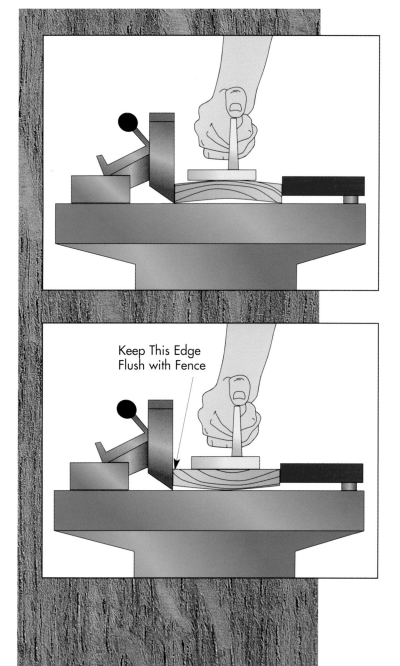

Keep This Edge Flush with Fence

JOINTER: ADJUSTMENTS

Many woodworkers think that just because a tool is made from cast iron, it will be perfectly flat and will always stay that way. Not true. Cast iron that's improperly cured can warp or twist over time. That's why it's important to check your tables periodically to make sure they're flat. Lay an accurate straightedge along the length of each bed, and check for gaps with a feeler gauge (*top photo*). Any gaps over 0.010" should be addressed. A reliable machine shop can regrind the surfaces flat, and some manufacturers provide this service.

Winding sticks

In addition to checking to make sure your tables are flat, it's a good idea to also check them periodically for twist. The easiest way to do this is with a pair of shop-made "winding sticks" (*middle photo*). Place the sticks on one table about an inch or two in from each edge. Then sight along the sticks at a low angle to check for twist. If you detect a twist, you may be able to correct it with shims; *see below*. If these don't cure the twist, the table will need to be reground.

Outfeed table alignment

It's also critical that the infeed and outfeed tables be parallel to each other. To check this, first raise the infeed table up to match the height of the outfeed table. Then lay a long, accurate straightedge along both tables and check to see if they're level. Quite often one of the tables will droop or sag. Most jointer manufacturers recommend adjusting the gibs to bring the table back into alignment; *see the bottom drawing* and check your owner's manual for detailed gib-adjustment procedure. In some cases this won't work and you'll have to insert machinist's shims between the table and the base to remove the sag or droop.

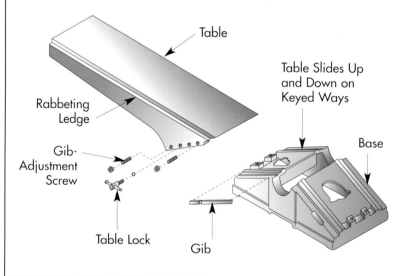

Adjusting Jointer Knives

Many woodworkers feel that some form of magic is required to adjust jointer knives accurately. Granted, they can be tricky—but all it really takes is a scrap of wood and a lot of patience. The sequence described here—adjusting the knives with a stick—has been around as long as jointers have been made. It's surprisingly accurate, and the patience is required mainly because of the inherent movement that's caused by adjustments to tighten things down.

Typically, when a screw or bolt is fully tightened, it causes the part that it's being tightened against to shift or twist. Even a slight movement can throw knife alignment off. And this is where the patience comes in. Adjusting the knives on a jointer is very straightforward, but it does require a lot of back and forth adjusting—set the knives, check them, loosen and readjust, check them again, readjust.... You get the idea.

Set fence

To use the stick method for adjusting jointer knives, start by unplugging the machine. Since you'll likely be adjusting the knives because they've been sharpened, take the time to clean the slots and locking bars with mineral spirits. Then insert a knife and locking bar, and tighten the nuts or screws so they're just friction-tight—that is, they're held in place but can still be adjusted. Next, slide the jointer fence to one side of the table (*top drawing*).

Mark stick

Select a scrap of reliably straight wood that's a foot or so long, and place the stick on top of the outfeed table so that it butts up against the fence and extends past the cutterhead and over the infeed table (*bottom drawing*). Then make a mark on the stick where it touches the edge or beginning of the outfeed table.

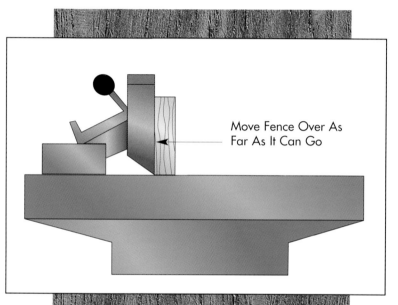

Move Fence Over As Far As It Can Go

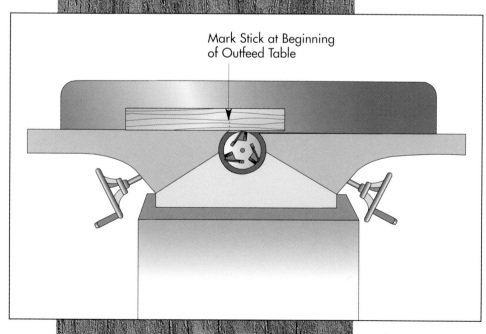

Mark Stick at Beginning of Outfeed Table

Rotate cutterhead

Now comes the fun part. Rotate the cutterhead forward by hand (don't grab the cutterhead to do this—instead, rotate it by moving the drive belt) so that it lifts up the stick and drags it forward slightly (*top drawing*). If the knife doesn't touch the stick, adjust it up so that it does. What you're looking for here is about $1/8$" of movement. This means that the cutterhead is roughly 0.003" above the outfeed table. If it drags the stick more than that, it's too high and needs to be adjusted down.

Make second mark

Once you've got the knife adjusted at one end so that it lifts and drags the stick about $1/8$", make a second mark on the stick where it touches the beginning of the outfeed table (*middle drawing*). These two marks then define the arc of the cutterhead at the desired height. If all the knives lift and drag the stick the same distance (on both ends), the knives are in perfect alignment.

Reset fence

After the knife is set on one side, slide the fence over to the other side of the table (*bottom drawing*). Then place the stick against the fence so the first mark you made touches the beginning of the outfeed table. Rotate the cutterhead and check to see whether the stick is dragged the same length. Odds are that it won't and that you'll need to adjust the knife. Use a scrap of wood to force the knife up or down and then recheck. Then tighten the locking bar and recheck with the stick. Adjust, tighten, and recheck, and repeat as necessary (patience, patience, patience...).

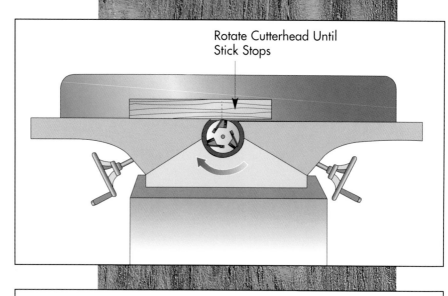

Rotate Cutterhead Until Stick Stops

Make Second Mark at Beginning of Outfeed Table

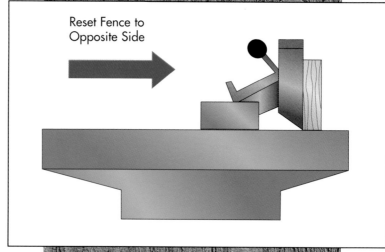

Reset Fence to Opposite Side

USING A DIAL INDICATOR

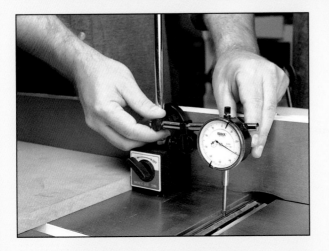

Setup

For the utmost in accuracy, you can use a dial indicator, like the one shown in the *top photo*, to adjust your jointer knives. Although it takes a bit of time to set up, you can adjust your knives in thousandths of an inch. I like to clamp a square scrap to the outfeed table *as shown* in order to keep the dial indicator in the same reference point along the table. An optional magnetic base allows you to firmly anchor the indicator in place.

Adjust one end

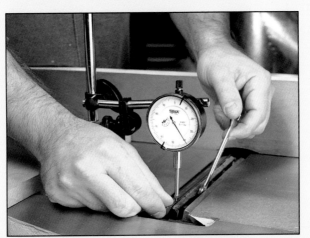

Adjust the position of the indicator so that the knives will be set the height above the table recommended by the manufacturer. With the tip of the indicator resting on the knife at top dead-center, loosen the gib bolts or screws to be friction-tight and then adjust the position of the knife so that the indicator reads the desired setting (*middle photo*).

Move to other end

Release the magnetic base of the dial indicator and slide it along the scrap to the other end of the table (*bottom photo*). Adjust the knife as you did for the first end. Slide the indicator back to its original position, check to make sure the knife didn't slip out of position, and adjust if necessary. Continue sliding the indicator back and forth, checking knife height until it's correct. Then tighten the gib screws or bolts, working from the center toward the ends. Repeat for the remaining knives.

TYPES OF PLANERS

Regardless of a planer's size, they all work similarly. A workpiece placed on the bed of the machine is fed in until it's gripped by the infeed roller (*top drawing*). This presses the stock against the bed and pushes it into the cutterhead. On heavy-duty planers, a bar called a chip breaker in front of the cutterhead breaks off chips and helps direct them out of the planer. Larger planers also employ a pressure bar after the cutterhead to hold the stock against the bed and prevent it from lifting up. The outfeed roller grips the stock and pulls it out, and some planers have rollers set into the bed to help reduce friction.

Bench-top

Although bench-top planers (*middle photo*) do a reasonable job of creating a smooth finish, they do have some drawbacks. Unlike their heavy-duty cousins, they don't use a serrated metal infeed roller. Instead they use rubber rollers, which don't grip rough lumber well and often skip or stall when dressing rough-sawn stock. However, as planers evolve, manufacturers strive to improve finish, reduce snipe, and add features that make these a solid investment.

Stationary

Choosing between a portable and a stationary planer can be confusing because stationary planers (*bottom photo*) can have cutting capabilities similar to a portable planer's, but cost twice as much. Although it may appear that they do the same job, it's like comparing a mini pickup with a full-sized truck. Yes, they can both haul a set amount of weight—but which one will hold up better working day in and day out? The full-sized truck, of course, because it's built with a heavy workload in mind. Stationary planers are similarly designed. In addition to using a powerful induction motor instead of the weaker universal motor, the internal parts of a quality stationary planer are beefier, often heavy cast iron, and are machined to closer tolerances.

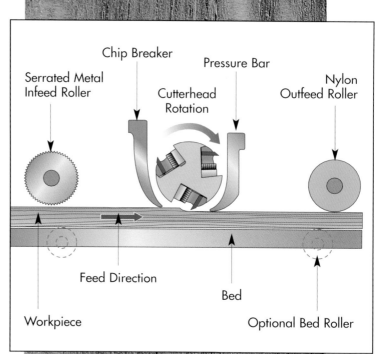

PLANER FEATURES

Bed width

Bed width is an important consideration when looking for a planer. As I mentioned previously, you can find both bench-top and stationary planers with similar capacities. Shown in the top photo are two planers: a 13" stationary planer/molder (*left in photo*) and a 12" bench-top planer (*right in photo*). Here again, although the width capacity is similar, the stationary jointer will hold up much better under heavy use.

Infeed and outfeed tables

Another important feature that's often overlooked is the planer's infeed/outfeed tables. There are three common setups: solid tables (*left in the middle photo*), tables with rollers (*right in the middle photo*), and rollers-only. I prefer solid tables on bench-top planers, and rollers-only on stationary models. Whichever type you choose, just make sure that it's easy to adjust them up and down for proper alignment.

MULTIPURPOSE MACHINES

Jointer/Planer

My first shop was the second bedroom in a single-wide mobile home—tiny, to say the least. With such limited space, I took a hard look at multipurpose machines. One of the first tools I purchased was the Inca jointer *shown at right*. Granted, it had a short bed; but it fit my space, the bed was wide ($8^5/8$"), and it came with an optional "thicknessing" attachment. The thicknessing attachment slipped onto the infeed table and did a surprisingly good job—although it didn't have a power feed. Instead, it relied on good old muscle power to feed the stock through. I built a lot of furniture with this machine and still use the jointer for smaller projects. A number of manufacturers continue to sell jointer/planers, most often in an "over and under" configuration, where the jointer on top and the planer below share a common cutterhead.

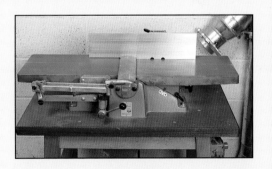

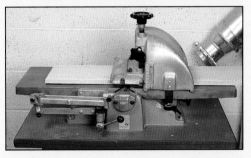

Knife changing

Just as with a jointer, changing knives on a planer can be a hassle. With this in mind, it's worth the time to investigate the knife-changing procedure for the planer you have in mind. Some of the bench-top planer manufacturers have gone to double-sided disposable knives that can be flipped when one side dulls, and thrown away when both are dull (*top photo*). Replacement blades are fairly inexpensive and often very easy to replace. The knives in stationary planers are often spring-loaded and are best changed with the aid of a magnetic setting jig (*see opposite page*).

Motor size

Motor size is a fair indication of the planer's power. For universal motors (like the one shown in the *middle photo*), ignore the horsepower rating and look for the amperage rating of the motor (in this case, 15 amps). Generally, the higher the amperage, the more powerful the motor. The horsepower ratings on induction motors are fairly accurate, but check the label for the wiring class of the motor—it should be at least a "B" ("F" is superior). Many import motors are not rated at all or have the lowest class ("A"). A motor with a poor wiring class will overheat quickly and need to be replaced.

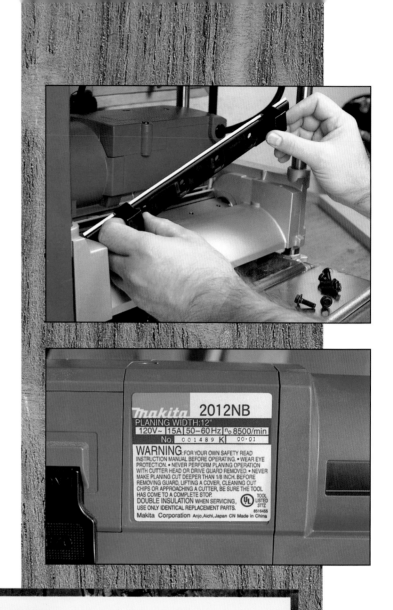

PLANER RECOMMENDATIONS

Choosing a planer is a bit more complicated than selecting a jointer, as there are more choices involved. The first step again is to look at what type of work you expect to do. If you're planning on surfacing rough-sawn lumber, go with a stationary planer and make sure it has a serrated metal infeed roller. Also, if your woodworking requires a lot of planing, you'll be better served with a stationary planer. If you're going to purchase a larger machine, consider investing in at least a 15" planer with a large dust-collection port (5" to 6" diameter) and a closed base.

If you work primarily with surfaced wood and your woodworking is limited to nights and weekends (like most of us), a quality bench-top planer will get the job done. Look for a model with adjustable infeed/outfeed tables, a strong motor, easy-to-adjust controls, and disposable knives that are simple to change or replace. Also, new advancements in planer design have greatly reduced snipe—look for this when you shop.

PLANER ACCESSORIES

Outfeed rollers

Regardless of the length of a workpiece you're planing, if it's not supported properly, it can tilt or pivot up or down so that the cutterhead ends up gouging the workpiece. This incident is referred to as "snipe" and is extremely common when working with planers. One way to help prevent this from happening is to fully support the workpiece throughout the entire cut—here's where outfeed or support rollers come to the rescue (*top photo*). Although any solid table at roughly the same height as the planer tables will do to support the workpiece, rollers work best because they provide frictionless support. And the more rollers, the better, since they will support a longer portion of the workpiece and help prevent it from dipping or twisting.

Dial calipers

If you don't own a dial caliper, buy one. I realize that this is a pretty strong statement, but you'll be glad you did. A dial caliper is one of the most accurate ways to precisely measure the thickness of stock—and they're incredibly easy to use (*middle photo*). I started using a dial caliper about 15 years ago and have used one on every project I've built since then. If you've ever struggled with a metal ruler or a tape measure, trying to accurately measure the thickness of a workpiece, you'll really appreciate a dial caliper.

Knife-setting jigs

Because of cramped spaces, I find planer knives even more of a hassle to adjust than jointer knives. Fortunately, tool accessory manufacturers have developed magnetic knife-setting jigs for planers, like the ones shown in the bottom photo. It's important to note that these knife-setting jigs are designed for specific-diameter cutterheads—the ones shown here can handle most portable planers but are too small for a stationary planer.

SQUARING STOCK

Although the sequence shown here for squaring up stock is no secret, it is one of the foundations of successful woodworking. If you don't start with square stock, virtually nothing else you do with the stock will work out right. Joinery won't fit, you'll experience gaps in your glue joints, and your projects won't hold up well over time.

Although I've said it previously, it bears repeating: None of the wood you buy will be perfectly square or flat. Just because a board is surfaced on all four sides doesn't mean it's square. Most likely it will be thicknessed accurately, but it won't be flat or square. The only way to ensure it's square is for you to make it so. The sequence shown here is the quickest, easiest way to get square stock for your woodworking projects.

Flatten one face

The first step in squaring up stock is to joint one face smooth (*top photo*). Use a push block (or two), and press the workpiece firmly against the infeed and outfeed tables as you make the cut. Remember to never pass your hands directly over the cutterhead, and to shift your weight to the outfeed table once the stock has passed the cutterhead. Don't worry about keeping the edge perfectly flush with the fence—you'll clean it up in the next step.

Square up an adjacent edge

After one face is jointed flat, the next step in squaring stock is to joint an edge

perpendicular to the flattened face. Press the jointed face up firmly against the fence, and take a series of light cuts until the entire edge is jointed flat (*bottom photo*). Here again, you'll want to shift your weight to the outfeed table once the stock passes over the cutterhead.

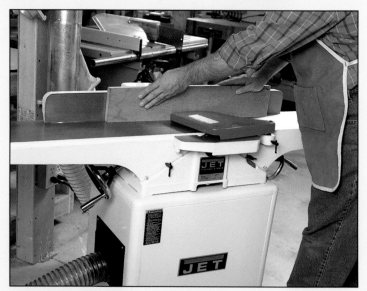

Make the faces parallel

Now that you have two flat perpendicular edges, the next step is to make the faces parallel to each other. The best tool for this job is the planer. Place the flattened face against the bed of the planer, adjust for a light cut, and feed the board into the planer (*top photo*). Let the infeed roller take over and push the board past the cutterhead. When it comes out the other side, lift the end of the board lightly to help prevent snipe.

Trim the remaining edge

With the faces parallel and one edge perpendicular, all that's left is to square up the remaining edge. In most cases, you'll want to rip the board to rough width on the table saw (*middle photo*). Then follow this up with a light pass or two over the jointer to bring the board to final its width and also to remove any saw marks.

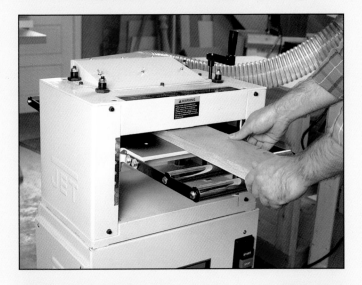

SQUARING STOCK SEQUENCE

1	**2**	**3**	**4**
JOINT ONE FACE	JOINT ADJACENT EDGE	THICKNESS-PLANE OPPOSITE FACE	RIP TO WIDTH

PLANING THIN/SHORT STOCK

For some time now, there's been a heated debate concerning the safety of planing thin stock. On one side, manufacturers claim this is hazardous, and they all list the minimum thickness you can safely plane on their planers—typically $1/2$". On the other side are woodworkers, who often need thinner stock. Although most manufacturers have built-in stops that limit how close the cutterhead can come to the planer's bed, woodworkers commonly get around this by using a sled, which allows the cutterhead to be closer to the workpiece (*see the sidebar on the opposite page*). Be warned that thin stock can explode in the planer with this method. If you choose to try this, make sure you don't stand directly behind or in front of the planer. Wear safety glasses and take light cuts.

Using a sled

One of the most common ways to plane thin stock is to attach it to a simple sled with double-sided tape (*top photo*). For best results, you should apply tape over the full length of the stock. If you don't, the rollers and cutterhead can flex the piece, resulting in an uneven cut. To adjust the depth of cut when using a sled, I recommend that you insert the sled with workpiece attached into the planer with the power off and lower the head until it just contacts the stock. Then back it off a quarter-turn, remove it, and begin planing (*middle photo*). Although I always suggest that you take light cuts, it's really important here—especially with

STAGGERED CUTS

Here's a slick way to avoid snipe when planing multiple pieces. SAFETY NOTE: This technique is safe only when all pieces are of identical thickness; if some are thinner, they won't be captured by the rollers and could kick back when they come in contact with the cutterhead. The way this works is simple. By feeding the stock into the planer so they're staggered (*photo above*), you keep the infeed and outfeed rollers constantly under tension, just as if you were planing a long board. Since snipe occurs only at the start or finish of a cut, it can occur only on the first and last pieces fed into the planer.

highly figured woods that tend to shatter when planed too thin. You'll have best luck with cuts less than $1/16$", preferably $1/32$" to $1/64$".

Short stock

Somewhere in the numerous warnings in your planer's manual is a note about minimum length of stock that can be safely planed. Make a note of this, and be sure to follow the manufacturer's recommendations. In an emergency, there is a way you can safely plane shorter stock: Just temporarily attach a pair of runners to the sides of the stock to be planed, as shown in the top photo. Just make sure the runners are thicker than the stock. This way they'll span the space between the feed rollers, allowing the stock to pass safely.

PLANER SLEDS

There are two common ways to plane thin stock on a planer: using a sled that hooks onto the planer's bed, and using a sled that you feed through the planer. The advantage of a hook-on sled is that you can plane multiple pieces easily. The disadvantage is that a hook-on sled does not support the stock to be planed as well as a feed-through sled when the workpiece is taped to the sled.

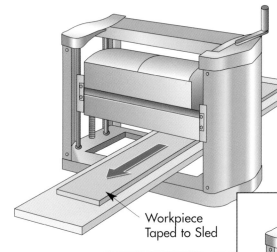

Workpiece
Taped to Sled

Feed-though sled: With this type of sled, the stock is attached to the sled with double-sided carpet tape and the sled/stock is fed through the planer.

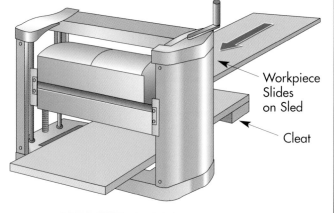

Workpiece
Slides
on Sled

Cleat

Hook-on sled: A hook-on sled has a cleat on the front edge that hooks onto the bed of the planer. The stock slides on the sled through the planer.

KNIFE-SETTING JIGS

Magnetic setting jigs for the planer work on the same principle as those for the jointer. A set of strong magnets are held in a plastic or metal head that fits the curve of the cutterhead. A third magnet in the jig holds the knife in position while you tighten the gib screws or bolts. On the jig shown here (*top drawing*), correct placement is achieved by butting the plastic leg of the jig up against the edge of the cutterhead.

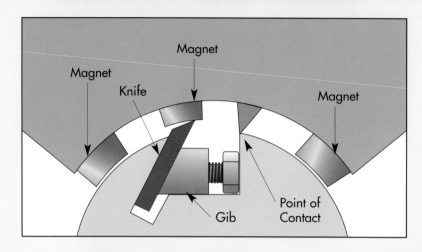

Magnet

Magnet

Knife

Magnet

Point of Contact

Gib

Remove hood

The first step in using a magnetic knife-setting jig for the planer is to unplug the planer and then remove the dust hood or chip deflector to gain access to the knives (*middle photo*). In most cases, the hood or deflector is held on with a pair of thumbscrews. CAUTION: The exposed knives are very sharp; exercise extreme caution when working around these. It's also a good idea to clear away any dust or chips with a blast of compressed air or with a vacuum.

Loosen gib screws

Once you've gained access to the knives, the next step is to loosen the gib screws or bolts that press the gib into the knives to hold them in place in the cutterhead (*bottom photo*). Note: If your planer uses elevating screws to adjust the height of the knives, back these off so that they don't interfere with the operation of the magnetic jig; consult your owner's manual for more on this.

Remove the gib and knife

With the gib bolts or screws loose, you should be able to lift out the gib (or locking bar, as it's sometimes called). Insert the tip of a screwdriver under one of the gib screws or bolts and pry the gib up—the gib should come up easily, and if it doesn't, double-check to make sure that all the bolts are sufficiently loose. Once the gib is out, carefully lift out the knife (*top photo*).

Clean gib slot

Now that the gib and knife are removed from the cutterhead, take the time to clean out the slot. Remove any sawdust or chips with compressed air or a vacuum, and follow this with a clean, dry cloth (*middle photo*). If you notice any pitch or resin deposits, dampen the cloth with some lacquer thinner or mineral spirits and scrub the slot clean. Clean the gib and knife as well before re-installing them.

Adjust knife

Insert the gib in the slot and slip in the knife. Adjust the gib screws or bolts until they just barely hold the knife in place. Position a magnetic knife-setting jig at each end of the cutterhead, following the manufacturer's directions. Press down on the jig so that the magnets grip the cutterhead and the knife. Tighten the gib bolts or screws in small increments, working from the center of the knife to the edges, until the knife is held securely in place (*bottom photo*). Repeat this process for the remaining knives.

SELF-ADJUSTING PLANER KNIVES

I've changed a lot of planer knives over the years, and I've never come across a system that's as quick and easy to use as the self-adjusting system that Makita features in their newest portable planer (*top photo*). From start to finish, they make this often-frustrating job a snap. They've thoughtfully engineered this planer to make changing knives a coffee break job instead of an all-day fiasco: A built-in cutterhead lock, double-sided knives, a long-handled socket wrench (to keep your fingers away from the sharp blades), magnetic holders that both grip and align the knives, and a retaining bracket that automatically locks the blades in the perfect position are just some reasons knife changing is so easy on this planer.

Loosen mounting bolts

To change the knives on the Makita planer, start by unplugging the machine, and then loosen the thumbscrews that hold the chip deflector in place and remove it. Then remove the right side cover and rotate the cutterhead until it automatically locks in position with the mounting bolts facing up. Now you can use the long-handled socket wrench provided to loosen the mounting bolts (*middle photo*).

Lift out the knife

Place the two magnetic holders supplied on the set plate, and push them forward until the small claws on the end contact the knife. Remove the installation bolts, and then grip the magnetic holders and raise them straight up (*bottom photo*). The knife can then be flipped end for end to expose a fresh edge (or replaced if both sides are dull) and realigned by setting the edges 1mm ($3/64$") past the plate. Reinstall the magnetic holders, and slip the heel of the set plate into the slot in the cutterhead. Reinstall the mounting bolts—and you're done.

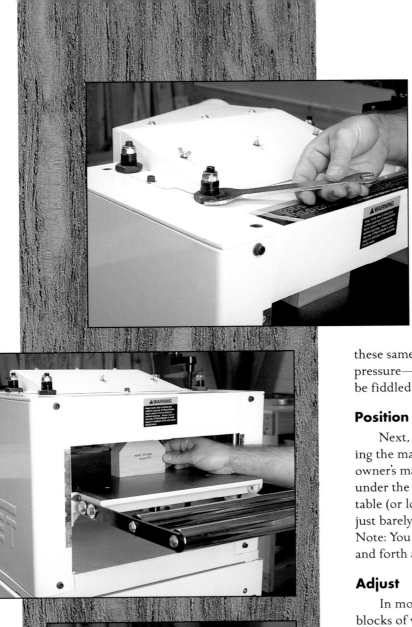

PLANER: ADJUSTING ROLLERS

Loosen locknut

On some planers, particularly planer/molders, you can adjust the feed-roller pressure to compensate for different operations and types of wood. To adjust the feed rollers, start by loosening the jam nuts that lock the rollers in position (*top photo*). Note that on these same posts are nuts that control the spring pressure—these are factory-set and should not be fiddled with.

Position gauge block

Next, make a reference guide block, following the manufacturer's instructions in the owner's manual. Then insert this guide block under the center of the feed roller and raise the table (or lower the cutterhead) until the roller just barely touches the block (*middle photo*). Note: You should be able to slide the block back and forth along the full width of the feed roller.

Adjust

In most cases, you'll have multiple guide blocks of varying heights designed for specific operations. Adjust the feed rollers by turning the threaded bushings on the posts, as shown here (*bottom photo*). Then slide the desired guide block under the feed roller. Here again, it'll be adjusted correctly when you can just barely slide the guide block back and forth along the entire length of the feed roller. Retighten the jam nuts and recheck; repeat this procedure for the outfeed roller.

Planer Snipe

Snipe occurs when the end of a workpiece lifts up into the spinning cutterhead. The resulting dished cut is so prevalent on most planers that many woodworkers think it's normal (*top photo*). It has become so accepted that many woodworkers routinely cut their boards an extra 6" to 8" long so that they can cut off the snipe on both ends. What a waste of time and good wood. As with snipe on a jointer, snipe on the planer can be caused by an improperly adjusted machine, or by using incorrect technique—both of which can usually be remedied (*see below*).

Feed rollers out of adjustment

Snipe on the planer is often caused by a pressure bar or outfeed roller that's set too high (*middle drawing*). In either case, the workpiece can tilt or spring up into the cutterhead once the trailing edge of the workpiece passes out from under the infeed roller. Check your owner's manual for the recommended adjustment procedure, and make the necessary adjustments.

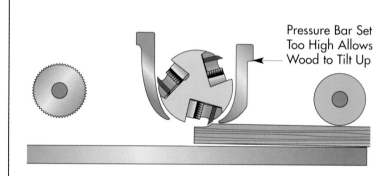

Pressure Bar Set Too High Allows Wood to Tilt Up

No support

Another common cause of planer snipe is not supporting the workpiece throughout the entire cut. Basically, the workpiece tilts on the table edge and the end of the board lifts up into the cutterhead (*bottom drawing*). Snipe can occur at the beginning of the cut as well as at the end if it's not supported. A good set of well-adjusted infeed and outfeed tables will go a long way to preventing this from happening. Outfeed rollers (*see page 95*) can also be used to support the workpiece to reduce the likelihood of snipe.

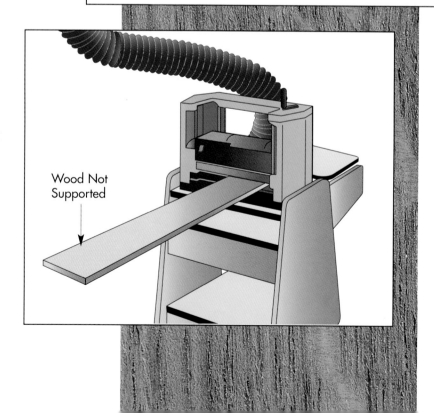

Wood Not Supported

PLANER CHIP-OUT

Sometimes, even when your knives are sharp, your dust-collection system is working, and the wood isn't highly figured, you can still experience chip-out like that shown here (*top photo*). That is, small chips are torn out of the surface of the wood as it passes under the cutterhead. When this occurs, there are a couple things to check: You may be feeding the wood into the planer incorrectly, or the pressure bar may be out of adjustment (*see below*).

Wrong direction

If you feed the wood into a planer so that the grain is slanting up toward the cutterhead (*as shown in the middle drawing*), the knives will chip out the unsupported wood fibers on the surface. When you feed wood into the planer, the grain of the wood should always slant down and away from the cutterhead. Since grain often changes direction within a piece of wood, feed the wood in so that the majority of the grain slants down and away, and take lighter cuts.

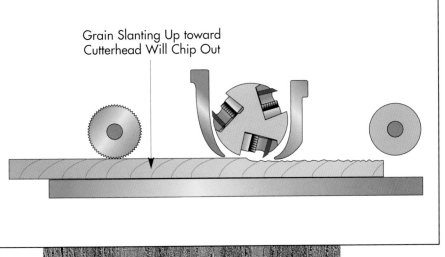

Grain Slanting Up toward
Cutterhead Will Chip Out

Chip breaker out of adjustment

If your planer has an adjustable chip breaker and you're experiencing chip-out, it may be that your chip breaker is set too high (*bottom drawing*). If it's not down pressing against the workpiece, it can't support the fibers being cut in front of it, and chip-out will occur. Consult your owner's manual for the recommended procedure, and make any necessary adjustments.

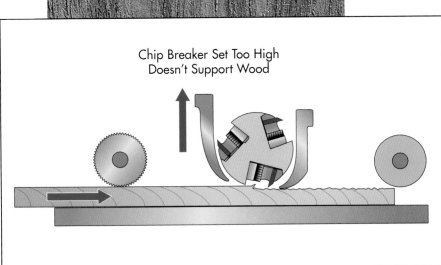

Chip Breaker Set Too High
Doesn't Support Wood

PORTABLE POWER PLANERS

 A power planer is basically a motorized hand plane. Most are capable of removing anywhere from $1/64$" to $1/16$" of wood in a single pass—without the elbow grease needed to operate a hand plane. Blade widths vary from 4" to almost 5"—more than enough to handle most jobs. All feature an adjustable depth of cut, and most come with grooves in the base to make chamfering (trimming the edge of a board at a 45-degree angle) a snap. Costs range from around $40 up to $150; you can also pick one up for a day at most rental centers for around $15.

Depth of cut

The first thing to do with a power planer is to adjust it to the desired depth of cut. As always, I'd recommend taking a series of lighter cuts, instead of one heavy cut. The cut of most power planers is adjusted by turning a large knob on the front of the planer to the depth indicated on the scale (*top photo*). Most power planers have a "zero" or "P" (for "park") position that sets the knives up into the planer so they don't protrude at all. The knives should be in this position whenever the planer is not in use.

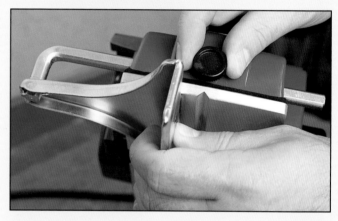

Fence

Quality power planers will come with a fence that can be used with the planer to make accurate cuts and rabbets (*see opposite page*). An auxiliary fence is also a good way to add extra support to the planer for almost any cut (*middle photo*). Just slide the fence into the desired position and tighten the lock knob. Then butt the fence up against the side of the workpiece and make the cut.

Support

Whenever you need to plane a narrow strip of wood, it's a good idea to add some additional support to the piece to prevent the planer from

tipping sideways during the cut. The simplest way to do this is to clamp a wide scrap of wood (like the 2×4 *shown in the bottom photo on the opposite page*) to the side of the workpiece. This creates a stable platform for the planer, and you'll get a smoother, more accurate cut.

Rabbet

One of the features I like best about a portable power planer is that it's extremely easy to cut accurate rabbets (*top photo*). Here's where a solid auxiliary fence comes in handy. Adjust the fence to match the desired width of the rabbet, and take a test cut on a scrap piece to make sure it's the correct width. Then adjust the planer for a light cut, and make a series of passes until the desired depth of the rabbet is reached.

Bevel

Bevels are also easy to create with a power planer (*middle photo*). The only problem here is that since you don't have an adjustable-angle fence, you need to lay out the angle carefully on both ends of the workpiece and stop frequently to see how you're doing. Note that even with careful layout, it's tough to cut an accurate bevel. With a little ingenuity, you may be able to fasten an angled fence to the planer to guide it for a more precise cut.

Chamfer

In addition to rabbets and bevels, one of the things a power planer excels at is cutting quick chamfers (*bottom photo*). Most power planers have a groove running the length of their base designed especially for this. This V-groove will ride along the edge of the workpiece and will press up against adjacent sides to create a very nice chamfer. This is one situation where you can safely take a deeper cut, as you're removing much less wood. As always, it's a good idea to make a test cut on a scrap piece first.

"Our first aim in making this new Machine was to insure more perfect and uniform work than could be done by hand... as a result we have the Invincible Sander—one which requires no expert or high-priced man to operate, and one that when adjustments are to be made can be done with accuracy, ease and dispatch."

YATES-AMERICAN MACHINE (1918 CATALOG)

POWER SANDERS

Of all the power tools on the market, the one group that sees constant improvement is power sanders. Every time I attend the National Hardware Show, I see a batch of new sanders, each claiming to produce more "perfect and uniform work" than the other. Why? Because everyone hates sanding. And everyone wants a better way to get it over with.

Sanding is tedious and messy; I have yet to meet a woodworker who says he or she enjoys it. Fortunately, power sanders make this necessary task less annoying. Thanks to new developments in these tools, especially the random-orbit sander, you can sand quickly, aggressively, and without thought to grain direction. Eventually, manufacturers will produce that truly "invincible" sander described by the Yates folks nearly a century ago.

No matter which model you use, it will always be important to match the sander to the job—some are very aggressive. You can quickly ruin a project with a belt sander: It's capable of dishing out a flat surface or rounding over a delicate detail in the blink of an eye. But you can tame these potentially destructive machines with proper maintenance, adjustment, and technique.

A trio of timeless power sanders (*from top to bottom*): an unusual 3-wheeled Craftsman 3" belt sander, model number 207.22301; a Powr-Kraft model number TPC8550A dual-motion sander (provides both orbital and in-line action); and a Craftsman sander-polisher, model number 110.7820.

TYPES OF POWER SANDERS

There are more kinds of power sanders out there than any other type of power tool. To name just a few there are orbital sanders, disk sanders, drum sanders, random-orbit sanders, detail sanders, belt sanders, stationary sanders... the list goes on.

Basic types

Although there are many kinds of sanders available, there are really only three main types, which can be categorized by their sanding action. A sander moves sandpaper in one of three basic motions: in circles, back and forth, or in a single direction.

Circular motion

Sanders that move an abrasive in a circular motion are orbital sanders and random-orbit sanders. These sanders accept square, rectangular, or round sheets of sandpaper. The size of the circular orbit determines the aggressiveness of the sander. Small orbits remove stock slowly, while larger orbits remove stock more quickly. (*See pages 111–112 for more on orbital sanders.*)

Back-and-forth motion

Sanders that provide a back-and-forth sanding motion are often referred to as in-line sanders. In the past, these were also known as finish sanders. Unfortunately, many modern tool manufacturers refer to their orbital sanders as finishing sanders, making the term *finish sander* obsolete for referring to in-line sanders. Back-and-forth sanding most closely approximates hand-sanding and is the ideal way to finish a project (*see page 113 for more on this type of sander*).

Single-direction sanding

With few exceptions, the bulk of the remaining sanders move an abrasive sheet in a single direction—usually by rotating a continuous abrasive belt around a drum, or by rotating a sanding disk. Portable belt sanders, stationary sanders, and drum and disk sanders all offer single-direction sanding. The odd duck is oscillating drum sanders, which both rotate a drum and move it up and down (*see page 124 for more on these unique machines*).

ORBITAL SANDERS

For years, orbital sanders (commonly called jitterbug sanders) were the mainstay in woodworking shops (*top photo*). They're reliable, leave few swirl marks, and are inexpensive. Although I do reach for my random-orbit sander for most sanding jobs (*see page* 112), an orbital offers a number of advantages. Because it's not as aggressive as a random-orbit, it's easier to use in confined spaces, and its square pad allows you to reach into corners (like inside a drawer or all the way into the back of a shelf). Their less-aggressive action also makes them ideal for delicate jobs where finesse is required.

Tiny orbits

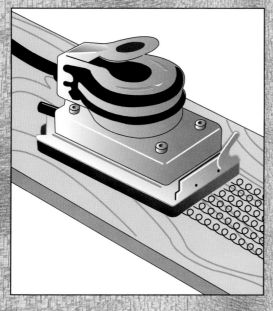

Although the tiny orbits of an orbital sander are preset by the amount of offset between the sanding pad and the motor shaft, the pattern that the sander produces depends on how fast you move the sander (*middle drawing*). The orbits are so small, you don't usually see them. The first time I did, it was disastrous. I was smoothing the final finish on a table and came across a "clinker"—a particle on the sandpaper larger than the rest. It scratched a clearly defined pattern on the tabletop similar to this drawing.

Pay attention to grain direction

Because an orbital sander's sanding action is a set pattern (that is, it's not random), it's important to pay attention to the grain of the workpiece. Always sand with the grain (*bottom drawing*). If you sand against the grain (or cross-grain), the sander will leave tiny swirls that will show up clearly when a finish is applied, particularly a stain, as the pigment will darken the cross-grain scratches. This takes a bit more patience than a random-orbit sander, and I suggest stopping about $1/4$" to $1/2$" away from a joint line where grain direction changes, and sanding this area by hand.

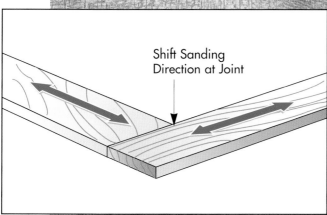

Shift Sanding Direction at Joint

RANDOM-ORBIT SANDERS

Of all the power sanders out there, the random-orbit is my favorite (*top photo*). Its unique sanding pattern (*middle drawing*) lets you sand wood while virtually disregarding grain direction. Because of this, it's terrific for leveling joints where the grain of the parts is perpendicular (like a frame-and-panel door). Also, these sanders chew through material fast, whether it's leveling a table top, or smoothing a final coat of finish. Note: Always start a random-orbit sander with the disk in contact with the surface; doing otherwise can cause swirl marks.

Unique sanding pattern

A random-orbit sander is sort of a hybrid of a disk sander and an orbital sander. It combines the large swirling motions of a disk sander with the smaller orbits of a jitterbug sander (*middle drawing*). The secret to creating a random pattern has to do with an offset cam that connects the drive motor to the sanding disk. As the disk moves over the surface, the sandpaper attached to the disk grabs the surface, causing the offset to engage and swirl the disk in a totally random pattern.

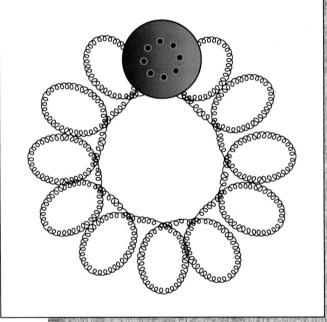

Ignore the grain

I have to admit it took me a while to get used to using a random-orbit sander. I was weaned on orbital sanders and had a hard time learning to ignore the grain. But that's exactly what you can do with a random-orbit sander (*bottom photo*). You can sand in any direction (although I still tend to follow the grain) and gleefully cross joint lines without worry. Because of their random action, these sanders will at first seem a bit "torquey"—that is, they tend to twist your wrist a bit when you first turn them on. This is normal, and after a while you won't even notice it.

IN-LINE SANDERS

In-line sanders (often referred to as straight-line sanders) are becoming harder and harder to find—particularly in a portable electric version. What you can still find is the air tool version, like the one shown here (*top photo*). That's because they're still very popular in auto body finishing, which relies heavily on pneumatic tools. The reason they're becoming hard to find is that they're being steadily replaced by the random-orbit sander. That's too bad, because the sanding pattern produced by an in-line sander most approximates hand-sanding.

Sanding pattern

An in-line sander uses a back-and-forth motion that is similar to hand-sanding (*middle drawing*). The big difference is that the stroke is only about $1/2$". Although not as aggressive as random-orbit or orbital sanders, these tools provide the ultimate in smooth, flat surfaces. ShopTip: If you do need to remove material fast, try angling the sander to the work surface as you would a belt sander (*see page 118 for more on this*).

Paper

In-line sanders use long strips of sandpaper (typically 9" to 17") that are held in place with built-in clamps (*bottom photo*). Some tool manufacturers sell conversion kits for their sanders so they'll accept either hook-and-loop or pressure-sensitive adhesive sandpaper. In most cases, you'll find a better selection of grits at an auto body supply store. I recommend aluminum oxide paper, as it will last much longer than garnet (*see pages 126–127 for more on sandpaper types and uses*).

Drum Sanders

A drum sander is a rubber cylinder with an arbor running through it that, when tightened, expands to grip a sanding sleeve. Drum sander sizes vary from $1/2" \times 1/2"$ up to $3" \times 3"$. When shopping for these, pay extra for a longer set; not only do these allow you to sand thicker materials, but also the larger sanding surface helps your sanding sleeves last longer since you can distribute wear and tear over the entire length of the sanding sleeve.

In a portable drill

For sanding curved parts, nothing beats a drum sander. The only trick to using a drum sander in a portable drill is to move the drill in the opposite direction the drum is spinning (*top drawing*). If you sand with the rotation, the drum will grab the workpiece and run along the edge out of control. To use the full length of the sanding sleeve, guide the drum gently in and out along the edge as you sand.

In the drill press

There are two major differences when using a drum sander in a drill press instead of on a drill (*middle photo*). First, you're presenting the workpiece to the drum sander. Here again, it's important to move the workpiece in the opposite direction the drum is spinning. Second, to sand the full width of a workpiece, you'll need to either insert the drum sander in a base with a hole in it or flip the workpiece periodically.

On the lathe

Drum-sanding on the lathe is made possible by the nifty pneumatic drum shown in the bottom photo. The sanding sleeve fits over an inflatable core. The advantage to this is that you can make the drum as stiff or as flexible as you want by varying the amount of air you pump into the core. The drum has a pin on one end to fit into the lathe's tailstock, and crossed notches on the drive end to fit a standard drive center on a headstock. These are available from most turning and woodworking mail-order catalogs.

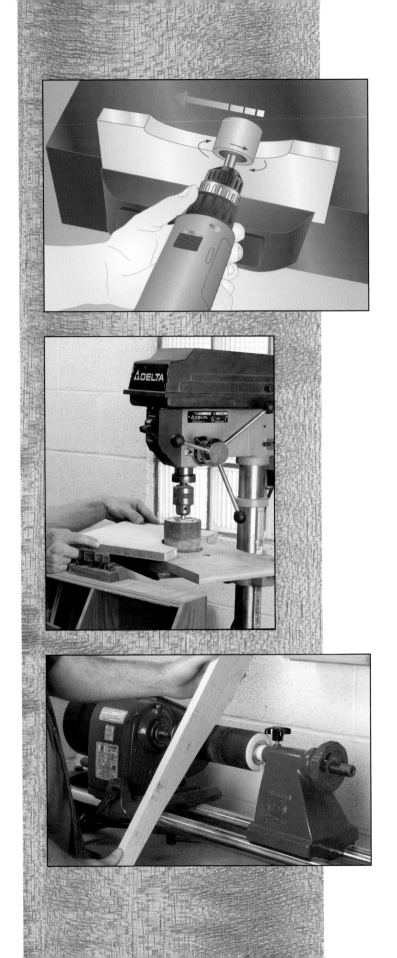

Photos courtesy of Freud Inc.,
copyright 2001

DISK SANDERS

A disk sander for portable drills is just a rubber disk (with an arbor) that accepts pressure-sensitive adhesive (PSA) sandpaper. All disks are not the same—a thin rubber disk is very flexible. This is great if you're sanding a curved surface. But if you're working on a flat surface, you'll be better off with a rigid disk. Another thing to look for is a dimpled surface: You'll find it's easier to remove PSA sandpaper from this than from a smooth and shiny disk.

For portable drills

The secret to disk-sanding is to hold the pad as flat as possible on the surface, use light pressure, and keep the sander moving continuously (*top photo*). If you stop in one spot, you're guaranteed to leave swirl marks. Even worse, if you're using a coarse grit, the disk will dig in and gouge the work.

For table saws

Numerous tool manufacturers sell metal disks that mount on the arbor of your table saw, just like a blade, and accept PSA sanding disks (*middle photos*). The metal disks are available in either 8" or 10" diameter and in a variety of bores to match your saw. The sanding disks range in grits from 80 to 220. The only problem I've had with these is that I find the saw motor speed too fast for sensitive sanding jobs. The high speed and fairly aggressive grits have a tendency to take material off quickly. This is good if you have a lot of material to remove, but not so great for fine sanding.

For the lathe

You can make your own sanding disk for a lathe by attaching a circle of MDF (medium-density fiberboard) to a faceplate with screws. Then apply a PSA sanding disk to it, and you're ready to go (*bottom photo*). The advantage with a lathe is that you can slow down the speed for controlled sanding. For sanding other than freehand, make a stand to fit over the lathe's bed, and clamp it to the top so it's about $^1/8$" to $^1/4$" away from the sanding disk.

PROFILE SANDERS

Profile sanders, like the one shown in the top photo, are a relatively new development in power-sanding. Unlike orbital sanders, a profile sander uses an in-line or back-and-forth sanding motion (*middle drawing*). This motion sands without removing critical details that a swirling motion would obliterate.

The beauty of this sander is that it accepts a wide variety of rubber pads (*see the sidebar below*) to get at those hard-to-reach spots. Most profile sanders also come with square or diamond-shaped pads for reaching into corners. The model shown here is supplied with two diamond-shaped pads: One is set to accept hook-and-loop sandpaper, and the other is designed for PSA (pressure-sensitive adhesive) paper. Some are also available with pad holders, where the pad can be mounted in two positions: standard, and offset for recessed areas requiring extra clearance. Most sanders are available as either single- or variable-speed.

Not for heavy sanding

Although these sanders do a good job of getting into hard-to-reach spots, they're not really designed for heavy sanding—and they're best used on bare wood. If you try to remove paint or other finishes, you'll discover that the paper quickly clogs. I use my profile sander only for touch-up work. You'll also find that PSA paper has a hard time sticking to the rubber pads in use—even if you use the manufacturer's paper (which is not cheap). I've found that keeping the pads super-clean helps. I wipe a pad with rubbing alcohol whenever I change paper to remove any dust or residual adhesive.

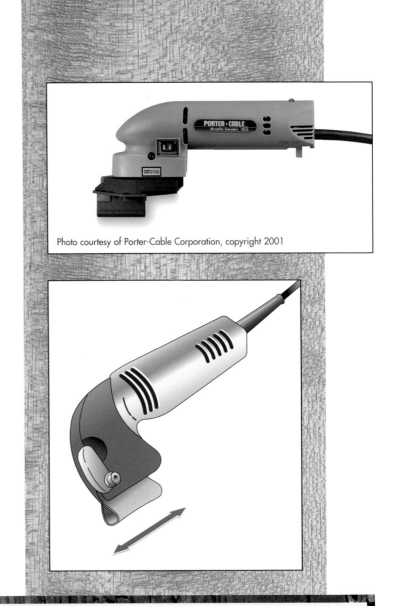

Photo courtesy of Porter-Cable Corporation, copyright 2001

PAD STYLES

The profile sander shown in the bottom photo comes with six convex pads, six concave pads, and five angled pads. Replacement pads are available, and I'd recommend purchasing a couple of spare 90-degree pads so that you can custom-shape them (they cut easily with a utility knife) to fit a particular profile.

DUST COLLECTION

Surprisingly, some of the biggest dust producers (and biggest mess makers) in a woodshop are portable sanders. That's because they're difficult to hook up to a dust collector. They are, after all,

supposed to be portable. But that's not to say that you can't capture the dust they produce. The two most common ways to do this are built-in filters and optional attachments for your shop vacuum.

Built-in filters

Portable power sanders are by far the most prolific users of built-in dust collection. Shown (*top photo*) are two common filter arrangements: a cylindrical filter that, although solid in appearance, has tiny holes to allow air to flow through it while still capturing dust, and a box-type filter that uses a fine mesh screen to capture dust. The advantage of the box type is that it typically has a larger storage space for dust, so you can use it longer without having to stop to empty the filter.

Vacuum-assist

Another dust-capturing option that's available for some power tools is vacuum-assisted collection (*middle photo*). In most cases, a special fixture or adapter is attached to the tool and is then hooked up to a shop vacuum or dust-collection system. Although it's fairly efficient, using a tool with an attached hose can be quite cumbersome. Vacuum-assist works well on belt sanders, as they generate such a large volume of dust in such a short time that they would overwhelm a built-in filter; a vacuum can handle the load.

Sanding tables

Sanding tables or downdraft tables are a great way to capture sanding dust. A sanding table is basically just a hollow box connected to a dust-collection system. Holes or slots in the top of the box make it easy for the collector to pull in wood dust for filtering (*bottom photo*). Sanding tables are particularly useful for sanding small parts, as the dust easily slides off the part for collection. They are not as good for sanding large panels and case goods, since the dust tends to lie on the panel, making collection difficult.

BELT SANDERS

I'll be honest and tell you up front that I don't use a belt sander much anymore. When I first got started in woodworking, it seemed like the best tool for smoothing panels and correcting problems. Over the years I've learned to prevent many of the problems by starting with square stock (*see pages 96–97*) and learning to take my time. And since I've learned to sharpen hand tools, I tend to reach for a hand plane to remove excess stock instead of grinding it away with a belt sander. A plane is quieter, there's less chance of a screw-up, it's less messy, and to me, it's more satisfying. On the plus side, belt sanders are capable of removing a lot of stock fast. Too fast, sometimes. It's amazingly easy to gouge or groove a workpiece with one of these beasts, although sanding frames (*see the sidebar on page 119*) go a long way toward "taming" them.

Adjust tracking

Even quality belt sanders have a hard time keeping the rotating belt "tracking" properly—that is, preventing it from slipping to one side or another. All belt sanders have a built-in adjustment knob that needs regular tweaking to keep the belt in line (*top photo*). If you notice that a particular belt slips a lot, your wheels may be dirty (*see page 120*) or the belt may be defective.

Skew to remove material fast

For general-purpose sanding, you should sand with the grain to prevent cross-grain scratches. If you want to remove a lot of material fast, you can skew the sander, much as you would a hand plane (*middle photo*). This is best done with a medium- or fine-grit belt, as a coarser belt will tend to leave deep cross-grain scratches that can be a real bear to remove.

Finish-sand with the grain

When you've finished removing the bulk of the waste from a workpiece, switch to sanding with the grain (*bottom photo*). Continue sanding

like this, changing belts to finer grits until the desired surface is achieved. For the final pass, I suggest using an orbital sander, or better yet, a random-orbit sander, followed by hand-sanding.

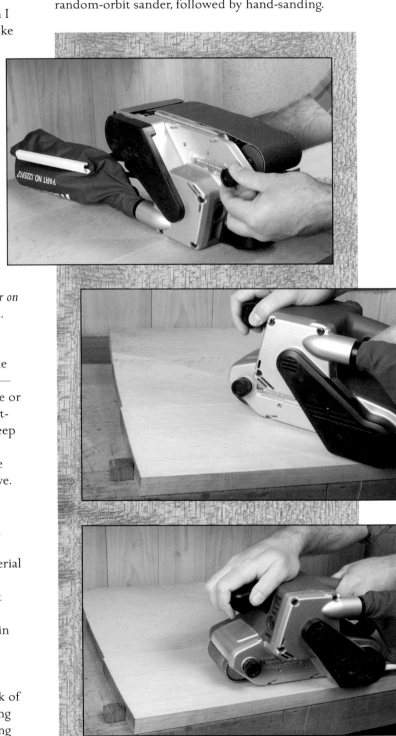

Keep the sander moving

If there's one cardinal rule in using a belt sander, it's to always keep the sander moving. Since these machines are able to remove material so quickly, they'll easily dish out a workpiece in a fraction of a second (*top photo*). As long as you keep the sander moving, either back and forth or from side to side, you can prevent this from occurring. And using a sanding frame (*see the sidebar below*) is an even more reliable way of preventing this.

Upside down for small parts

If you don't have a stationary sander like those shown on pages 122–123, you can use your portable belt sander to handle some of the tasks by flipping the sander upside down (*middle photo*). There are a couple ways to do this. Some sanders (like the one shown) have flat tops, so you can just invert it and set it on the bench. Other manufacturers offer stands that hold their sanders (some horizontal, some vertical).

SANDING FRAMES

Sanding frames are sort of like training wheels for a belt sander. The sides of the frame support the sander and prevent the user from tipping it to one side or another (*bottom photo*). And like training wheels, they also prevent nasty accidents (dished cuts, grooves, etc.) by never allowing the sander to remove stock without support—something that's all too easy with a belt sander by itself. Most sanding frames connect to the belt sander by way of a pair of brackets that attach to the sides of the sander. What really makes these nice is that you can set the depth of "cut" by turning an adjustment knob on the frame. This allows you to dial in how much stock you want to remove. A word of caution here: For the sanding frame to work, all four edges of the frame need to be in contact with the work surface. If they don't, the sander can tilt—just like a kid's bike with only one training wheel.

Belt Sander Tune-Up

With regular use, all belt sanders need to be tuned up to maintain their level of performance. This is simply a matter of cleaning followed by a couple of quick adjustments.

Remove the belt

Start by removing the belt. On most sanders this is accomplished by holding the sander at an angle on the bench with the front wheel touching. Then push the sander into the bench top until the spring-loaded front wheel "catches" in its back position. Once the tension is released, you can slip off the belt (*top photo*). Other types of belt sanders have a built-in lever that releases the tension (*see the top drawing on the opposite page*).

Check the platen

Once the belt is removed, remove any dust with a blast of compressed air or with a vacuum. Then check the platen that the belt rides across. This metal plate can develop rust (like the one shown in the middle photo), which you should remove with emery cloth or other abrasive. Check to make sure there isn't excessive wear near the ends, and replace the platen if necessary (consult your owner's manual for part information and replacement directions).

Check the wheels

Next, check the wheels to make sure they're clean and free from residue (such as gum and pitch from softwoods, or glue residue). Remove any of this with mineral spirits or lacquer thinner (*bottom photo*). Also, remove any rust deposits with emery cloth. What you're looking for here is clean and flat. Note that some belt sanders have grooved wheels. If yours does, make sure that there's nothing trapped in the grooves—a toothbrush dipped in mineral spirits works well to clean these.

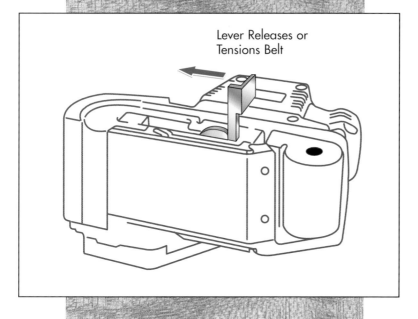

Lever Releases or Tensions Belt

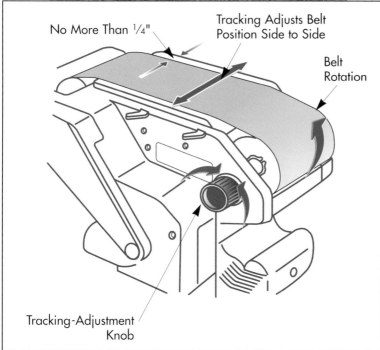

No More Than ¼"

Tracking Adjusts Belt Position Side to Side

Belt Rotation

Tracking-Adjustment Knob

After the belt sander is clean and dry, you can slip on a new belt. Although many new belts being manufactured are bi-directional—that is, you can put them on in either direction—many belts are still direction-sensitive and need to be put on so that the arrow (inside the belt) points in the direction of rotation.

Adjust the tension

Slip the new belt on, and release the front wheel or pull the lever back to re-tension the belt (*top drawing*). Spring tension is set at the factory, and most tool manufacturers suggest not tampering with it. And I agree. Too much tension and you'll be snapping belts regularly. Too little and the belt won't stay on or track. If you think your belt tension isn't correct, I'd suggest dropping the sander off at your local tool repair shop. Let the pros handle this one.

Adjust the tracking

With the belt in place and properly tensioned, all that's left is to adjust the tracking. In most cases, you're looking for the belt to cover the platen with the same amount of overlap on each side (*bottom drawing*). Some manufacturers specify the maximum amount the belt should be away from the edge of the sander body. Most tracking-adjustment knobs are on the side of the body and will be spring-loaded. It's spring-loaded so that it won't turn out of adjustment due to the vibration of the sander. If you do notice the tracking knob moving on its own, check to see whether you can increase the spring pressure, or replace the spring (consult your owner's manual for both of these options). Finally, if you notice that a belt is having problems tracking properly and it's a bi-directional belt, remove it and reverse it—sometimes this is all it takes.

STATIONARY SANDERS

If you can afford one (and have the available space), you'll find a stationary sander a very handy tool in the shop. Most stationary sanders, like the one in the top photo, are combination machines that offer a large belt (typically 6" × 48") and a nice-sized disk (often around 12" in diameter). A single motor drive both sanders, and quality sanders will have chutes either built-in or available separately to help collect dust—and these machines are capable of generating clouds of it. I find myself using my stationary sander most often for sanding parts to a layout line after rough-sawing them on a band saw or scroll saw.

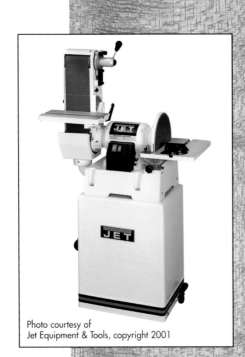

Photo courtesy of
Jet Equipment & Tools, copyright 2001

Tilting table

Make sure that the table on the stationary sander you're interested in tilts easily for sanding bevels (*middle photo*). Although most sanders will have a built-in angle indicator, you're always better off using this only for rough positioning, and then fine-tuning the table's position with a bevel gauge set with a protractor. Better sanders will have tables that securely lock in place on both sides to prevent one corner of the table from dipping lower than the other when sanding a heavy workpiece.

Belt positions

The sanding belt on most sanders is designed for two positions: horizontal and vertical (*bottom photo*). Often there's an intermediate stop at 45 degrees. Check to make sure that the belt is easily adjusted between positions and that it locks securely in place. On larger machines, all this typically requires is pulling out a stop and lifting the belt. With the smaller machine shown here, you need to loosen a clamp with an Allen wrench. Better sanders also offer a large sanding table for the belt versus the small metal bracket shown here.

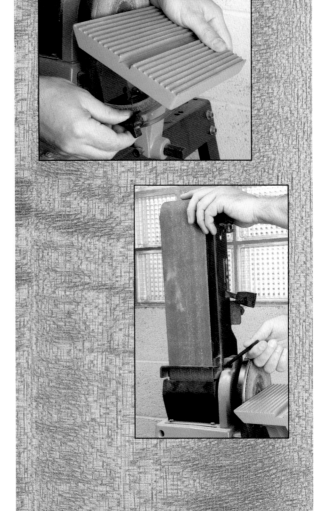

Replacing the disk

Sanding disks that fit on the round metal plate are held in place with pressure-sensitive adhesive (PSA). When a disks wears and it's time to replace it, start by peeling the edge of the disk back from the plate (*top photo*). Quite often, the disk won't want to come off—this is especially true for disks that have been on for a long time, or where used heavily. Heavy use tends to generate a lot of heat, which effectively "bakes" the adhesive on the plate. If this happens, drizzle a little lacquer thinner between the disk and the plate, and it'll peel right off. Also, make sure to remove all adhesive residue with lacquer thinner to eliminate lumps under the new disk and to achieve the best bond.

Tracking the belt

Just as with a portable belt sander (*see page* 121), the belt on a stationary sander will regularly need its tracking adjusted (*middle photo*). Tracking keeps the belt centered on the wheels and on quality sanders will need only occasional adjustment. If you notice that the belt has a tendency to slip out of adjustment regularly, remove it and clean the wheels. If this doesn't work, try another belt. Sometimes the belt itself is the culprit, if it wasn't manufactured properly—one edge of the belt is wider than the other, and no amount of adjusting will keep this belt tracked.

USING THE FENCE

I've always found the sanding belt fence to be quite handy (*bottom photo*). As long as it's set perfectly perpendicular to the surface of the belt, it's extremely useful for truing of parts. Since the rotation of the belt will pull the workpiece firmly into the fence, it's fairly easy to sand crisp 90-degree edges. The only trick is to use uniform pressure on the workpiece. A word of caution here: Even with a fine-grit belt, a stationary sander is capable of removing a lot of wood in the blink of an eye. Use light, even pressure and check your work often.

OSCILLATING DRUM SANDERS

If you've ever used a drum sander with a portable drill or on the drill press (*see page* 114), it probably didn't take long to learn that it's real easy to burn a workpiece. A the same time, you also likely discovered that the grit on the sanding drum where you were sanding wore off quickly. Both of these problems are eliminated with an oscillating drum sander (*top photo*). The unique dual-motion action of the sander provides aggressive sanding with minimal or no burning (*middle drawing*). The drums on oscillating drum sanders not only spin, but they also move up and down. This helps to keep both the drum and the workpiece cool and, at the same time, spreads out the sanding over a wider portion of the drum.

Oscillating drum sanders are available in three flavors: stationary (like the one shown in the top photo), smaller bench-top versions, and portable units (*see the sidebar below*). Most offer drums ranging in size from 1/4" up to 4". Sanding sleeves for the drums come in a wide variety of grits, ranging from fine to coarse. The drums either screw directly to the motor shaft, or slip over the shaft and are secured with a nut on top. For most shops, one of the bench-top versions will work fine.

Photo courtesy of Jet Equipment & Tools, copyright 2001

Drum Spins and Moves Up and Down

PORTABLE UNITS

Porter-Cable recently introduced a portable version of an oscillating drum sander. Why portable? There are plenty of jobs where it's a lot more desirable to take the tool to the work instead of the work to the tool—sanding the edges of a large project is awkward at best with a bench-top or stationary sander. Their portable unit lets you tackle those large projects with ease (*bottom photo*). It also lets you take on jobs that the other machines can't handle—interior sanding work, like sanding the edges smooth on a cutout. The unit shown here accepts 1/2" to 2" drums and with the aid of a special mounting plate can be converted to a bench-top sander.

Photo courtesy of Porter-Cable Corporation, copyright 2001

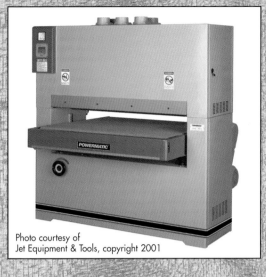

Photo courtesy of
Jet Equipment & Tools, copyright 2001

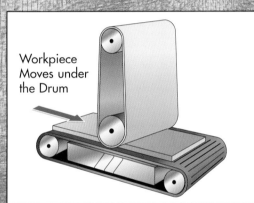

Workpiece
Moves under
the Drum

WIDE-BELT SANDERS

Although you'll rarely see a wide-belt sander like the one shown here (*top photo*) in a small woodworking shop, I've included it here because these often pop up in cabinet shops and school shops, where you may be able to rent time on one to tackle those heavy-duty sanding jobs. Wide-belt sanders are used to rapidly smooth wide panels—table tops, or even full sheets of plywood. The advantage they offer is that the workpiece can be sanded in a single pass to create a uniformly flat surface.

How they work

The large sanding belts on most wide-belt sanders fit large drums that are oriented vertically (*middle drawing*). The workpiece is pushed under the drum by way of a continuous-loop conveyer belt. How much material is removed depends on the position of the platen under the conveyer belt. These machines remove a lot of material quickly with a coarse belt, or leave a super-smooth finish with a fine-grit belt. If you get access to one, have someone familiar with the machine go over with you how to operate it.

HORIZONTAL DRUM SANDERS

A more realistic and affordable way to bring wide sanding capabilities into the small shop is with a horizontal drum sander (*bottom photo*). Unlike standard drum sanders, a horizontal drum sander doesn't use sanding sleeves. Instead, a strip of abrasive is wrapped around the drum, much like the stripes on a barber pole. Just as with a wide-belt sander, the workpiece is pushed under the drum via a conveyer belt.

An item to note here: Dust collection is mandatory with these machines. Without it, the workpiece will heat up, clouds of dust will fill the shop, and the machine's moving parts will quickly load up with dust and eventually fail. Also note that because the dust is so fine, you'll need super-fine filter bags on your system. I feel that 1-micron bags are essential to your long-term respiratory health.

Photo courtesy of Jet Equipment & Tools,
copyright 2001

SANDPAPER

No chapter about power sanders would be complete without discussing sandpaper. Like many woodworkers, I loathe sanding. It's messy work that I try to minimize. Whenever possible, I reduce hand- or power-sanding by using planes and scrapers. But unless a project consists mainly of flat, square surfaces (like many Craftsman-style designs), I end up using sandpaper for final smoothing.

Types of sandpaper

There are three main types of sandpaper that are commonly used in a woodshop: silicon carbide, garnet, and aluminum oxide (*top photo*). For years, all that was available was garnet sandpaper, made from finely crushed semi-precious stones. This type of paper tends to dull and wear out quickly but has the best reputation for smoothing without leaving scratches. Silicon carbide paper (often called wet/dry sandpaper) is used primarily for sanding between coats of finish, since it can be used wet. Aluminum oxide is a relatively new abrasive that stands up well and lasts much longer than garnet.

Regardless of the type of abrasive, all sandpaper is categorized by grits that define the size of the particle (*see the chart at right*). Although there are many rules of thumb for grit selection, I've found that I usually need only two for smoothing. I start with 150-grit and finish with 220. This is possible because I don't expect the sandpaper to do what I should have done with a plane or a scraper. Instead of grinding away at an imperfection with a power sander, I'll remove it first with a plane or scraper. Many woodworkers don't realize that it's actually faster this way.

SANDPAPER GRITS

Name	Specified Grit ANSI* CAMI**	Particle Size (microns)	Typical Uses
Ultra fine	600	16	Sanding a final finish
Extra fine	400	23.6	Sanding between coats
Extra fine	320	36	Sanding between coats
Very fine	280	44	Preparing surfaces for oil finishes
Very fine	240	53.5	Preparing surfaces for oil finishes
Very fine	220	64	Preparing surfaces for oil finishes
Fine	180	79	Preparing surfaces for varnish or polyurethane
Fine	150	95	Preparing surfaces for varnish or polyurethane
Fine	120	113	Preparing surfaces for varnish or polyurethane
Medium	100	136	Smoothing surfaces, sanding joints flush
Medium	80	189	Smoothing surfaces, sanding joints flush
Medium	60	266	Smoothing surfaces, sanding joints flush
Coarse	50	341	Leveling surfaces, removing stock
Very coarse	36	536	Grinding wood to shape, rough-surfacing
Extra coarse	20	886	Grinding wood to shape

*ANSI = American National Standards Institute
**CAMI = Coated Abrasive Manufacturers Institute

Wet/dry sandpaper

Silicon-carbide paper is often referred to as wet/dry sandpaper because it's one of the few sandpapers that can be used either way (*top photo*). I use it dry for getting wood as smooth as a baby's bottom, and wet for sanding between coats of a finish. Often I'll use a solution of water with a few drops of dishwashing detergent as a lubricant. Just make sure to wipe the piece thoroughly a couple of times with clear water and a clean cloth after sanding. Allow the project to dry, and apply the next coat of finish.

Micro-mesh

Originally developed for the airline industry to remove scratches in airplane windows, micro-mesh abrasives are the ultimate in sanding (*middle photo*). When I first learned about these years ago, I originally thought it was going too far. I mean really—sanding up to 4000 grit? But I've found that there are times when I am looking for the ultimate finish, particularly when I'm working with non-wood materials: brass, plastic, products like Corian. Micro-mesh allows me to create a glass-smooth finish that these materials can really show off. Micro-mesh abrasives are available from some mail-order woodworking catalogs.

PSA VS. HOOK-AND-LOOP

On power sanders of old, the sandpaper was attached to the sanding pad by way of a couple of spring-type clamps. These clamps gripped the ends of the sandpaper and did a fair job as long as the sandpaper didn't tear. Modern sanders use one of two improved ways to hold the sandpaper in place. The first improvement was PSA sandpaper (pressure-sensitive adhesive)—also known as peel-and-stick (*top photo at right*). The back of this paper is coated with adhesive that, once the backing is removed, adheres readily to a rubber pad. Unfortunately, it often sticks too well, and removing and replacing paper can be a chore. An even better development was hook-and-loop paper (*bottom photo at right*). This paper works like Velcro and is super-easy to remove and replace—plus it has the added benefit of being reusable.

"The Wood Shaper or Variety Molder is one of the essential machines to a wood working plant. The style of work varies from rabbeting, grooving and fluting to shaping of every description."

OLIVER MACHINERY COMPANY (1921 CATALOG)

ROUTERS and SHAPERS

I heartily agree with the Oliver Machinery Company. A router or a shaper is absolutely essential in the woodshop. Of all the projects I've completed in the last 20 years, I can't think of more than a handful that haven't called for a router at some point in their construction.

Many woodworkers see the router as purely an edge shaper, a tool to dress up the edge of a board with a round-over or an ogee. Certainly this is one of the most frequent and common uses, but this is the tip of the proverbial iceberg. I use my router for about 75% of my joinery. That's because unlike a power saw, which leaves saw marks, a router leaves crisp, flat-bottomed edges.

I reach for my portable router or table-mounted router regularly to cut box joints, locking rabbet joints, dovetails, grooves, dadoes... the list goes on. Did you know that you can even joint with a router?

When the talk turns to routers, "versatile" is the word most often used to describe this multi-use workhorse. The router was "one of the essential machines" in 1921, and it still holds true today.

The memorable Craftsman electric router shown here was common in woodworking shops a few decades ago, and many (like this one) are still in use today. This reliable router has a ¼" collet and a 6-amp motor and was made by Simpson-Sears (model number 315.25031).

TYPES OF ROUTERS

There are almost as many routers out there as there are drills—and that's a lot to choose from. But they all fall into three basic categories: standard routers, plunge routers, and laminate trimmers.

Standard routers

A standard router consists of a router base and a motor unit (*top photo*). The motor unit slides up and down or rotates within the base to adjust the depth of cut. Most are single-speed and because they have fewer parts than a plunge router, are generally more reliable. For handheld work, I prefer this type of router because its smaller size makes it easier to maneuver. A $1^1/2$-hp motor will handle most of the work you can throw at it. Look for easy, convenient adjustments (*see page 133 for more on this*) and smooth, heavy-duty castings.

Plunge routers

Plunge routers are similar to standard routers except that the motor unit slides up and down on a pair of spring-loaded metal rods (*middle photo*). The normal resting place of the motor unit is at the top of the rods. To make a cut, you release a lever and push down to lower (or plunge) the bit into the workpiece. This type of router excels at cutting mortises and is my tool of choice for mounting in a router table, as the depth-of-cut adjustment is easier to get to. If you're planning on mounting the router in a table, I recommend buying at least a 3-hp model with variable speed. You'll be glad you have the extra power when using large-profile bits that remove a lot of wood, such as vertical raised-panel bits.

Laminate trimmers

Although intended only for use to trim laminate edges when installing countertops, the diminutive size of laminate trimmers has made them a standard tool in many shops (*bottom photo*).

Photo courtesy of Makita USA, copyright 2001

Photo courtesy of Freud Inc., copyright 2001

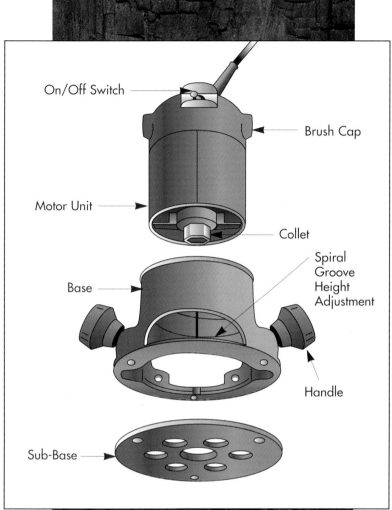

On/Off Switch

Brush Cap

Motor Unit

Collet

Spiral Groove Height Adjustment

Base

Handle

Sub-Base

That's because they can get into places where larger routers just can't. I find myself reaching for my laminate trimmer more regularly than my standard router for hand-held jobs. Their low weight and powerful motors (these little guys are surprisingly torquey) make them the perfect tool for a wide variety of routing challenges.

Router anatomy

A standard router (like the one shown in the drawing at left) has two main parts: a motor unit and a base. The motor unit contains the motor and drive shaft; the collet and/or collet nut attaches to the drive shaft to accept a bit. The motor unit contains the brush caps, which hold in the brushes. The on/off switch may or may not be contained in this unit, although it typically is.

The router base accepts the motor unit and offers some type of height-adjustment mechanism: a rack-and-pinion, a plunge mechanism complete with rods, or a pin-and-groove system where a pin on the motor unit engages a spiral groove inside the router body. There's also some type of locking mechanism to secure the motor unit in the base once it has been adjusted to the desired depth of cut. This typically involves a split router base that squeezes or clamps the motor unit when the locking knob or lever is activated.

The bottom of the base is covered with a plastic or phenolic sub-base that has a cutout for the router bit to pass through. This plastic base prevents the router from marring the surface of the workpiece. Handles on the sides of the router provide the means to guide it during the cut. Most router bases have some type of depth-of-cut indicator, but this should be used only for rough positioning—always make a test cut to sneak up on the final cut.

ROUTER FEATURES

Motor size

Although tool makers use various descriptors to indicate the "power" of a router (heavy-duty, industrial, etc.), the true indicator of a tool's power is its amperage rating. As a rule of thumb, the higher the amperage (noted on the side of the router in the top photo), the more powerful it is. The term "develops xx horsepower" is meaningless—it's just market hype; stick with the amperage rating.

Collet type and size

There are two main sizes of collets, and two different types. The size indicates the diameter of router bit shank that the collet can handle: either 1/4" or 1/2" (*left and right in the middle photo, respectively*). Savvy router manufacturers are beginning to ship their routers with both collets. I always recommend the stiffer 1/2" bits since they flex less and help reduce chatter and vibration. As far as collet types go, either the collet is split or the end of the motor shaft is split to grip the bit when the collet nut is tightened. Stick with a split collet: When it wears out, it's inexpensive to replace. When a split shaft wears out, you effectively need a new router.

Plunge capability

One of the primary features to decide on is whether you need plunge capability (*standard router at left in the bottom photo, plunge router to the right*). There are three good reasons to go with a plunge router over a standard: They allow you to safely make plunge cuts (such as when routing mortises), they're easier to adjust, and they're handier in a router table. If you're not planning on mounting the router in a table and you have no intention of routing mortises, a standard router will serve you well; otherwise a plunge router is your best bet.

Adjustment ergonomics

I always recommend that tool shoppers get their hands on a potential tool before buying it. This is the only way to determine whether the tools ergonomics and your hands are a good match. Take bit-height adjustment, for example. In the router at right in the top photo, the height lock is an easy-to-use snap-type lever. On the router at left, the locking mechanism is a paddle-style bolt in the rear of the router. Most people find the snap-lever easier to operate. The only way you'll know is to give it a try.

On/off switch accessibility

An important feature to look for in a router is how accessible the on/off switch is. Take a look at the three examples in the middle photo. On the router at far left, the on/off trigger is built into the handle. Although this is convenient, it's also a safety hazard since it's easy to turn on the router simply by picking it up. The on/off switch on the router at far right is safer because it's on top of the router, but it's not as convenient as the router in the middle. Here the switch can be easily toggled on and off with a flip of the thumb.

ROUTER RECOMMENDATIONS

I can't tell you how many times I've been asked, "What's the best router to buy?" I usually respond be asking them what they intend to do—use it mainly as a hand-held, or mount it in a table? I prefer a standard router or a laminate trimmer for handheld work and a plunge router for a table-mounted router. If you can afford to, buy both. If not, some manufacturers offer router kits that include a standard router with an optional base that converts it into a plunge router. I bought a setup like this from Porter-Cable and mounted the plunge base in my router table and keep the standard base on hand for handheld work. Since I leave the router motor unit mostly in the router table, all I have to do is unscrew it and set it in the handheld base as needed. The transition is quick and painless—quite a nifty system.

ROUTER BITS

It's kind of funny when you think about the fact that router bits are classified as an accessory. A router without a bit is like a computer without software—all you can do is plug it in and stare at it. There are two basic types of router bits available: unpiloted and piloted. Both types can be found made from high-speed steel (HSS) or with carbide tips. Don't waste your money on HSS—go with carbide. They cost more, but they'll stay sharper a whole lot longer. You'll also have a choice of ¼"- or ½"-shank bits. If your router will take ½" bits, I recommend always buying ½" shanks—the stouter shank helps reduce both flexing and vibration to provide a more accurate cut.

Unpiloted bits

An unpiloted (or nonpiloted) bit is any router bit that can make a cut in from the edge of a workpiece. As no means are provided to guide the bit, they can be used either freehand (such as when routing a name in a sign) or with the aid of an edge guide or straightedge (*see page 136 for more on this*). The most common types of unpiloted bits are straight bits, cove bits, veining bits, and dovetails bits (*top photo*).

Piloted bits

A piloted bit is any router bit that has a built-in guide. Virtually all bits that rout a decorative edge are piloted bits: round-over bits, cove bits, chamfer bits, and ogee bits, to name a few. The most common type of guide used today is the bearing. A bearing is mounted either below or above the cutter and rides along the edge of the workpiece (or template) to guide the cut (*middle photo*). The width of cut of some bits can be changed by changing the rub collar to a smaller diameter or by replacing the bearing with a different size. This is particularly common with rabbeting bits so that

you can cut a variety of rabbet widths with the same bit. When piloted router bits first hit the market, the guide was simply a rub collar that fit into the bottom of the bit (*bottom photo*).

Specialty router bits

In addition to edge-profiling bits and standard nonpiloted bits (such as straight bits), there are a number of bits available designed to make special cuts. Three of these that I use often are shown in the top photo. *From left to right*, a three-wing slot cutter, a spiral-end mill bit, and a keyhole cutter. A slot cutter is a piloted bit that allows you to easily rout slots or grooves in the edge of a workpiece. The advantage here is that the workpiece lies flat on the router table or workbench, and gravity works for you instead of against you. Spiral-mill bits are my choice for cutting mortises because the flutes of the bit efficiently pull chips out of the mortise. A keyhole bit routs a recessed slot for hanging pictures and cabinets. This is a nonpiloted bit that requires an edge guide for a straight cut.

Multi-profile bits

Multi-profile bits allow you to rout different profiles with the same bit (*middle photo*). This is possible because there are multiple cutters stacked on the same bit. Raising or lowering the bit presents a different combination of cutters to the workpiece. The one shown here will cut both halves of a cope-and-stick joint used for frame-and-panel work.

ANTI-KICKBACK BITS

Photo courtesy of Freud Inc., copyright 2001

Anti-kickback router bits are a new breed of bits pioneered by Freud (www.freudinc.com). What makes these bits different from ordinary router bits is the large body that wraps around in front of the cutter (*bottom photo*). What this does is limit the amount of cut under unsafe conditions, such as if you were to slip and push a workpiece into a spinning bit. With a conventional bit, the cutter would slam into the workpiece, take a huge bite, and fling the workpiece back at you—a nasty event called kickback. With an anti-kickback bit, the workpiece would hit the large body in front of the bit and take a much smaller bite, and the kickback (if any) would be greatly reduced. These work so well that I've gradually replaced all my conventional bits with anti-kickback bits.

ROUTER EDGE GUIDES

Unless you're doing freehand routing with a nonpiloted router bit, you'll need some form of guide to make a straight cut. The three most common ways to guide a nonpiloted bit in a router are to use an edge guide that attaches to the router, use a commercially made clamp-on straightedge, or use a shop-made straightedge.

Attaching an edge guide

Most router manufacturers make an edge guide for their routers that lets you make cuts a limited distance in from the edge—typically 6" to 10". They're most useful for routing grooves, dadoes, and flutes. Some edge guides come with the tool; others can be purchased as an accessory. They range in quality and cost from a metal bracket that slides on a pair of rods that slip into the router base, to elaborate extrusions that connect solidly to the base, like the Porter-Cable edge guide shown in the top photo. Quality edge guides will allow for both rough and fine positioning. Keep in mind that you can increase the stability of most of these by attaching a long "outrigger" to the edge guide itself.

Clamp-on straightedges

One of my favorite tool accessories of all time is a clamp-on straightedge (*middle photo*). These low-profile clamps securely hook on to the edges of the workpiece and allow the tool to pass over it without interfering with the cut. They're available in a variety of lengths and are well worth their cost.

Temporary edge guide

If you don't have an edge guide like those mentioned *above*, you can also clamp a straight piece of scrap wood to the router (*bottom photo*). The only problem with this method is that you're limited by the diameter of the sub-base, unless you make a larger one.

ROUTER TABLES

Photo courtesy of Porter-Cable Corporation, copyright 2001

If you've never mounted your router in a table, you're utilizing only half of its capabilities, maybe even less. Mounting a router in a table effectively turns in into a mini-shaper. You can accurately cut joints, work safely with small parts, and add a level of precision to your router work that may not have seemed possible. There's quite a variety of router tables on the market these days, everything from bench-top tables and stationary models to shop-made versions.

Bench-top router tables

For woodworkers with limited space, a bench-top router table makes a lot of sense (*top photo*). Just clamp it to your workbench and you're ready to go. When shopping for a bench-top model, look for heavy castings to help dampen vibration, and a fence that allows for rough and fine positioning. A dust chute is essential, as well as easy router mounting and removal.

Stationary router tables

If you've got the shop space, I'd recommend going with a stationary router table. The mass of a larger table not only helps dampen vibration, but it also puts the work at the correct height and saves you the hassle of setting up a bench-top unit (*middle photo*). I think you'll be surprised at how quickly a stationary router table will become one of your most used tools.

SHOP-MADE ROUTER TABLE

Although there are plans for a number of shop-made router tables on the market, my absolute favorite is the ShopNotes router table shown in the bottom photo. The original plans for this router table were published in ShopNotes magazine, Issue #1. It features a fully adjustable fence, bit storage, and a replaceable insert (*see the sidebar on page* 141) and can be made with either an open or closed base (the closed base is great at silencing the annoying whine a router makes). Plans are still available from ShopNotes project supplies at www.WoodsmithStore.com.

Photo courtesy of ShopNotes magazine, copyright 1992, August Home Publishing Company

ROUTER TECHNIQUES

For all its versatility, the router is an amazingly simple tool to operate. There are only a couple of rules to keep in mind, most importantly, routing direction and depth of cut.

Direction is important

The number one router rule concerns the feed direction—that is, how you move the router with respect to the workpiece. Since the router bit always rotates in the same direction (clockwise if you look at it from above), it's important to move the router so the bit will enter the wood correctly. When routing an outside edge, move the router counterclockwise; for an inside edge, move it clockwise (*top drawing*). If you move the router in the wrong direction (referred to as *backrouting*), you'll know immediately, as the router will tend to grab the workpiece and "run." Occasionally, backrouting has its uses; *see the opposite page.*

Stabilizing a cut

For a router to make an accurate cut, the router bit needs to be perpendicular to the face of the workpiece. The router base can handle this task on most cuts, especially when the full base rides on the workpiece (such as when routing a groove or dado). However, on edge cuts,

where one half of the base extends unsupported past the workpiece, the router can tip, ruining the cut. There are two ways to prevent this. One is to lay a scrap of wood the same thickness as the workpiece an inch or two away from the edge so the unsupported section can ride on it (*middle drawing*). Alternatively, you can use double-sided tape to attach a wood scrap "outrigger" under the unsupported section of the router base so it will move along with the cut.

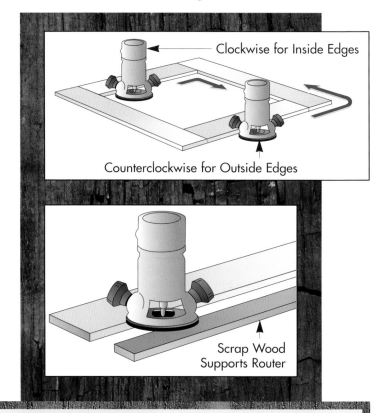

Clockwise for Inside Edges

Counterclockwise for Outside Edges

Scrap Wood Supports Router

TIGHTENING AND LOOSENING COLLETS

■ Over the years, I've watched many woodworkers struggle with the wrenches used to tighten and loosen most router collets. Typically they'll take a wrench in each hand and, with Popeye-like effort, tighten the collet or break it free and rap the knuckles together. The best way

I've found to avoid this is to use just one hand. Place one wrench on the spindle and the other on the collet so the wrenches are splayed slightly. Then squeeze to loosen or tighten (*bottom photo*). The pressure from one hand is all you should ever need to hold a bit. If more is required, it's time to replace the collet.

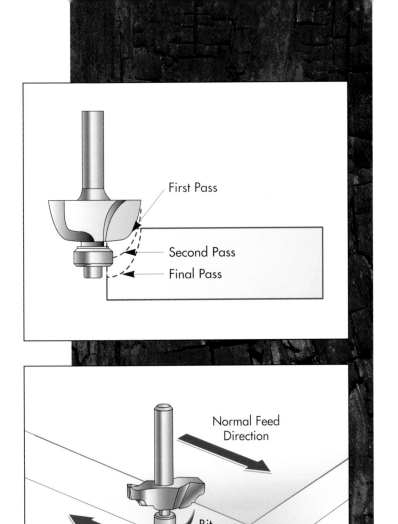

First Pass

Second Pass

Final Pass

Take multiple passes

Probably the most common mistake that I see beginning woodworkers (and even some seasoned veterans) make is to try to make a cut in a single pass. Although some heavy-duty routers are capable of this, there are a number of reasons why taking a series of lighter multiple passes is better (*top drawing*). First, a lighter cut tends to chip out less. Second, it's easier on the bit and router. Third, the cut is easier to control and will end up more precise, smoother, and with less burning. My general rule of thumb is to take three equal cuts to reach a full profile. Occasionally, I'll take three lighter cuts, and a final super-light cut for an extra-smooth finish.

Backrouting

Backrouting is a technique that can be used to help prevent chip-out. Basically, the router is moved *opposite* the normal direction so the cutting edge of the bit can't lift out slivers of wood (*middle drawing*). Backrouting is dangerous and should be attempted only after you feel comfortable with a router. That's because in backrouting, the bit won't pull itself into the wood as it normally does, and the router will tend to bounce along the edge. If you decide to try this, take light cuts and keep a firm grip on the router. DO NOT backrout on a table-mounted router—the router bit can grab the workpiece and pull it and your fingers into the bit.

Normal Feed Direction

Bit Rotation

Backrouting

ROUTER MATS

Routing small pieces has always been a challenge, as it's almost impossible to hold the workpiece securely without the clamps interfering with the router. The solution to this problem came from, of all places, the recreational vehicle industry. For years, the shelves of RVs were lined with special rubber mats that gripped the contents and helped prevent them from shifting on the road. Eventually a quick-thinking RV owner/woodworker figured out that these would do a great job of holding a small workpiece for routing—and they do (*bottom photo*). Nowadays, you can find "router mats" in every woodworking store and mail-order catalog.

ROUTER TABLE TECHNIQUES

With a table-mounted router, you present the workpiece to the router instead of the other way around. For setup, all you need to do is adjust the bit height and set the fence.

Adjust the bit height

How you adjust the height of the bit in your table-mounted router will depend on your router. I've found that plunge routers are the easiest to adjust because all you have to do is reach up and turn a knob (note that you can purchase extensions for most plunge routers that will bring the knob down so it's readily accessible). I generally use a small rule to roughly position the bit height (*top drawing*) and then make a test cut or two to sneak up on the final cut.

Set the fence

Once the bit height is set, you can turn your attention to the fence. If you're using a piloted bit, you can do without the fence, but I usually use it anyway and adjust it so it's flush with the bearing. This prevents those annoying little bearing tracks that a piloted bit can leave in the edge of a workpiece (particularly in softwoods). Note that the fence does not have to be parallel to the edge of the table—it can be at any angle, as long as the desired amount of bit is exposed (*middle drawing*).

Centering cuts

I've watched a lot of woodworkers spend a considerable amount of time trying to tweak the position of a router fence so that it'll make a true centered cut with a nonpiloted bit, such as a straight bit used to rout a groove or mortise. The easiest way I've found to get a perfectly centered cut is to use a narrower straight bit (for instance, I'll use a $1/4$" bit to make a $3/8$" groove) and take two

passes, flipping the workpiece end for end between cuts (*bottom photo*). This perfectly centers the groove, and all you have to do is make a couple of test cuts, adjusting the fence to produce the proper width.

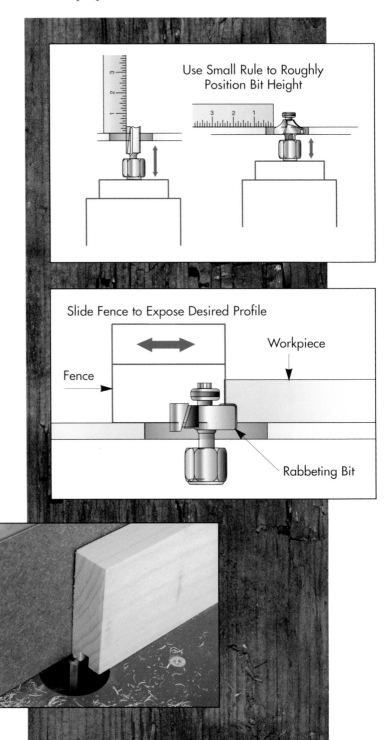

Use Small Rule to Roughly Position Bit Height

Slide Fence to Expose Desired Profile

Fence

Workpiece

Rabbeting Bit

Stopped cuts

A stopped or partial cut is a common task for which a table-mounted router is particularly well suited. Once your bit height and fence are set, all you need to do is clamp a scrap to the fence to limit the cut (*top photo*). To position a stop, make a pencil mark on your router table that defines the edge of the bit. Then mark the side of the workpiece where you want the cut to stop. Align both marks, and clamp a scrap to the fence so it butts up against the end of the workpiece. If you're cutting a mortise, you'll need two stops to define both ends, and the cut is made by butting up one end of the workpiece against one stop, lowering it onto the spinning bit, and then pushing it forward until it hits the other.

The router as a jointer

Yes, the router is so versatile, you can even use it to joint wood! The only limitation here is stock thickness. If you're using a standard straight bit, you'll be able to joint stock that's $3/4$" thick or less. Here's how it works. Attach a piece of plastic laminate to the outfeed side of your router table fence (*middle drawing*). Then insert a straight bit into the router (preferably a $3/4$" bit—its stouter width will help prevent it from bowing under the cut) and adjust the fence so the plastic laminate is flush with the edge of the bit. This effectively creates an infeed and an outfeed table just like a jointer, except that it's easier to handle large pieces since they lie flat on the router table instead of being held vertically as they would with a jointer.

TOP VIEW

Recess in Fence for Bit

Plastic Laminate Serves As Outfeed Table

Bit Rotation

Feed Direction

Workpiece

ROUTER TABLE INSERTS

One of the niftiest ideas I've seen for a table-mounted router is to attach the router to a plate that's recessed into the table top (*bottom photo*). This makes it easy to lift out the router to change and adjust bits (instead of crouching down under the table—the older you get, the more important this becomes!). Many woodworking stores and mail-order catalogs now offer premade router table inserts or offer materials to make your own. The one shown here is made from $1/4$" phenolic—a resin-based composite that's flat and tough and can be readily worked with any carbide-tipped tool.

SHAPERS

I'll tell you right from the start that I'm not fond of shapers. I had a rather harrowing experience years ago, the first time I used a shaper. Granted, much of it was caused by inexperience: I tried to take a full cut in one pass—and I was hand-feeding the stock. I was cutting a full round-over on a small tabletop, when halfway through the first cut, the shaper tore the panel (about 24" × 30") out of my hands and flung it across the full width of the shop in the community college where I was working. It shot the panel out with such terrific force that it stuck in the wall where it hit. Dazed and shaking, I shut off the machine and counted my fingers. Fortunately, they were all there (and still are).

A shaper is a potentially dangerous machine. But if you treat it with respect and use proper technique, it can do more than any table-mounted router. Shapers are capable of handling larger cutters (even custom cutters), and when used with a power feeder (*see below*), they can turn out a lot of work fast. Most shapers come with one or two interchangeable spindles that accept cutters with $^1/_2$" or $^3/_4$" bores (*top photo*). Some shapers also have optional router bit collets that accept $^1/_2$"- and $^1/_4$"-shank router bits. Most have multiple speeds and the motor can be reversed.

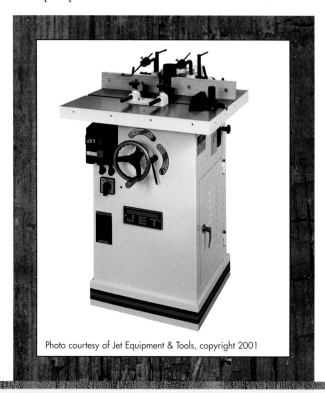

Photo courtesy of Jet Equipment & Tools, copyright 2001

POWER FEEDERS

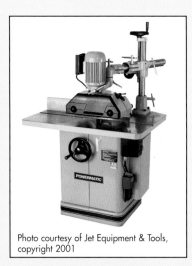

Photo courtesy of Jet Equipment & Tools, copyright 2001

■ Although many woodworkers think power feeders are only for use in industry, where they're trying to speed things up, a power feeder is also the number one safety device for a shaper. I'm a big fan of power feeders. I think that anyone who owns a shaper should have one. Anything that can keep your hands away from a spinning cutter is essential in my book. It wasn't until I used a shaper with a power feeder that I started to become comfortable with the shaper.

A power feeder attaches to the side of the shaper and utilizes a set of rubber wheels driven by an internal motor to grip and feed the workpiece past the cutter (*bottom photo*). In addition to speed and safety, power feeders also add precision to your shaping. They do this two ways. First, since the feed rate is constant, the cut is more consistent and burning rarely occurs (as long as the cutter is sharp). Second, besides pushing the workpiece past the cutter, it also presses it firmly against the fence and cutter, resulting in a more accurate cut than hand-feeding can accomplish.

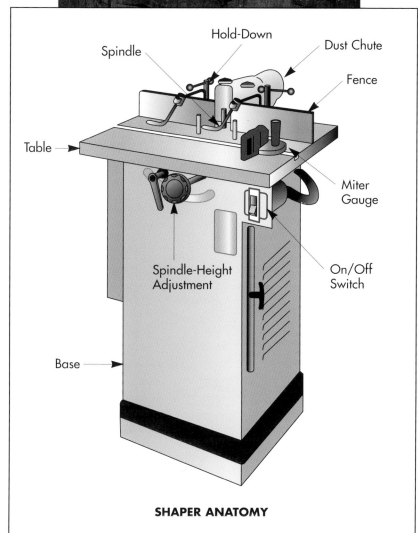

Spindle

Hold-Down

Dust Chute

Fence

Table

Miter
Gauge

Spindle-Height
Adjustment

On/Off
Switch

Base

SHAPER ANATOMY

Shaper anatomy

A shaper consists of four main units: a base, a table, a motor-driven spindle, and a fence (*top drawing*). The base may be open or closed, and it supports the table and motor-driven spindle. The table typically is cast iron and has a slot recessed in the top for a miter gauge. A motor-driven spindle accepts different-shaped cutters, and the spindle adjusts up and down via a handcrank and a locking knob on the side of the base.

The fence of the shaper is notched in the middle, or has separate halves to fit around the spindle. It usually is secured to the table top by way of a pair of built-in clamps. Both halves of the fence can typically be adjusted independently—often with a micro-adjusting knob.

Connected to the fence are hold-downs or featherboards that press the workpiece firmly into the table surface and the fence and cutter. If there's dust-collection capabilities, the dust chute or port is usually connected to the fence as well.

SHAPER TECHNIQUES

Installing cutters

Although not as quick as changing a bit in a router, changing a shaper's cutter is almost as simple. Most cutters are secured to the spindle by a locking nut that threads on top (*top photo*). Some shapers use a pair of wrenches to tighten the locking nut; others use a single wrench and a spindle lock. This is also the time to select and install the proper insert to fit around the cutter. Most systems use a series or set of inserts that fit into each other. Add or remove inserts so that there's a minimal amount of clearance between the perimeter of the cutter and the insert, but still plenty for the cutter to spin freely without making contact.

Setting the height

The height of a shaper cutter is adjusted by raising or lowering the spindle. In most cases, there's handcrank/locking knob that's similar to the blade-raising setup on a table saw (*middle photo*). The locking knob holds the adjustment in place during use. Loosen it and you can turn the handcrank to adjust the cutter. Note that just as with many table saw setups, you may need to hold the handcrank while you tighten the locking knob to prevent it from shifting the handcrank position (and cutter height).

SHAPER-CUTTERS

▨ Shaper-cutters are available in almost as many shapes and sizes as router bits (*bottom photo*). Quality cutters will have thick carbide tips and will be well-balanced. I tend to stay away from large-diameter bits like the red raised-panel bit in the bottom photo. The large circumference of these cutters generates amazing speeds at the outer edges and can be extremely dangerous. If you have to use a cutter this big, make sure to use a power feeder to prevent an accident (*see the sidebar on page* 142).

Adjust the fence

Unlike the fence on most table-mounted routers, the two halves of a shaper's fence can be independently adjusted. This allows you to shape any portion or the entire edge. Quality shapers will offer both rough and fine positioning of the fences. Once the fence is roughly positioned and clamped firmly to the table via the built-in fence clamps, you can fine-tune the position by moving a lever or turning a knob like the one shown in the top photo. For most cuts, you'll want the fences in line with each other. I just hold a metal straightedge across the fences and adjust them so they both butt up against it.

Use the guard and featherboards

Almost every shaper has a guard that fits over the arbor to keep your fingers away from the spinning cutter—typically it's a disk made of high-impact plastic. In addition to the guard, most shapers come with featherboards, which are used to keep the workpiece in firm contact with the cutter as it's fed past. Typically, there's a unit that presses the workpiece firmly into the shaper's table (*orange plastic bar in the middle photo*) and another unit (usually spring-loaded or spring steel) to press the edge of the workpiece into the fence and cutter (*curved black metal piece in middle photo*). All of these come standard for a reason—they make operating the shaper safer. Use them!

Take light cuts

Just as with the router, it's important to take light cuts with a shaper. Even though the larger shaper motor is capable of taking a bigger bite, you run into the same tear-out problems on a shaper as you do with a router. Lighter cuts mean less chip-out—and it's safer... and it's easier on the machine. My general rule of thumb is to take at least three passes, taking off a third each time (*bottom photo*). If I'm looking for a super-smooth finish, I'll remove a bit less on the first three passes and follow this up with a final light pass.

AIR
TOOLS

I started using air tools well over 25 years ago when I was in the service—mainly pressure washers and simple air nozzles to clean parts. You sure can get a lot of work done with compressed air, I found. Since then, I've used air tools to do everything from building walls with air nailers to cutting custom profiles on shaper knives with a die grinder.

Air tools have become increasingly popular as more people have discovered the same appeal that works for Mr. Maloof: a combination of power, precision, and efficiency. There are other advantages, too. Since air continuously flows through the tool, there's less chance for heat buildup, which means longer tool life. Most air-powered tools run more quietly than their electric cousins. And, air-powered tools generally weigh less.

Although air tools have been used for decades in manufacturing, they've gained widespread acceptance only recently. Now you'll often find a compressor in a workshop delivering power to nail guns, staplers, pressure washers, spray guns, drills...and maybe to your next project.

The two air nailers shown here were some of the first ever made. The TA tacker (*in the background*) was designed by A. G. Juilfs in the late 1940s. It was used to fasten head liners across the front windshield and back package shelf of automobiles. Shortly thereafter, the model AT (*foreground*) was developed for work on automobile door openings (*photo courtesy of Senco Products, Inc., copyright 2001*).

Types of Compressors

There are two basic types of compressors: oil-lubricated and oil-less. Both types have advantages and disadvantages.

Oil-lubricated compressor

Just like the engine in your car, an oil-lubricated compressor needs regular maintenance: Oil must be checked and topped off, and the filter and oil will need to be periodically replaced. Despite this, oil-lubricated compressors have a reputation for hardiness and dependability on the job site. They will often run twice as long as an oil-free compressor between rebuilds.

The typical oil-lubricated compressor consists of an air pump that's powered by either a gas engine or an electric motor, a tank to store the compressed air, and handles and/or wheels to make the compressor portable (*top photo*). There's also an air outlet to tap into the tank, a petcock to empty condensed water from the tank, and usually a built-in regulator and pressure gauge to adjust and monitor airflow. It's important to note that oil-lubricated compressors are splash-lubricated. This means that they must be run on a level surface. If the compressor is set up on a slope, the crankshaft won't splash enough oil onto the internal parts, resulting in accelerated wear and failure.

Oil-less compressors

Oil-free or "self-lubricated" compressors run without oil. Instead, they use nonmetal piston rings, Teflon-coated parts, and sealed bearings (*bottom photo*). In effect, they're maintenance-free—but only for a while: Since they don't use a lubricant, the internal parts of an oil-free compressor are constantly rubbing against each other. Also note that because of this, they have a tendency to be loud. On the plus side, since there's no oil to splash around for lubrication, you don't have to worry about keeping an oil-less compressor level—it can be used at almost any angle. Finally, since there's no oil inside the air pump, no oil can get into the air line to contaminate finishes.

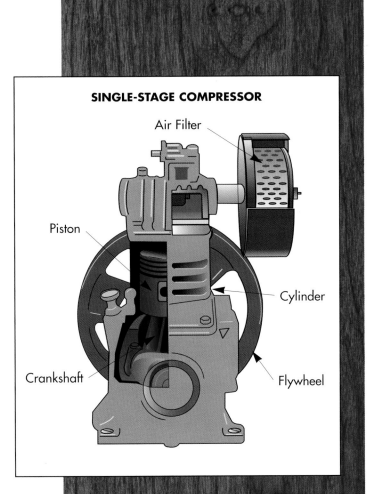

SINGLE-STAGE COMPRESSOR

Air Filter

Piston

Cylinder

Crankshaft

Flywheel

One of the things that can be confusing when you're looking to buy a compressor is to find two with the same horsepower rating but producing widely different airflows. This often has to do with the design of the compressor: whether it's single- or two-stage, or if it has one or more pistons.

Number of pistons

A single-stage compressor squeezes air in a single piston stroke to 25 to 125 psi (*top drawing*). In a two-stage, intermediate pressurized air is further compressed in a second cylinder to 100 to 250 psi (*bottom drawing*). Since most air tools require only 90 to 100 psi to operate, a single-stage compressor will handle just about any job you can throw at it. Also, two-stage compressors tend to be more expensive and heavier than single-stage units and usually require 220 volts.

In between single and two-stage compressors are double reciprocating compressors. Although this type of compressor sports twin pistons, they're still one-stage compressors, as they compress air in a single piston stroke. But with two cylinders, they squeeze twice as much air, resulting in double the air delivery.

A compressor works on the same principle as a bicycle tire pump. When a piston inside a cylinder is drawn back, it pulls air into the chamber. When the cylinder pushes forward, it compresses the air. The only difference with a compressor is the piston is powered by a gas or electric motor via a crankshaft. The motor runs until a certain pressure is achieved in the tank (typically 110 to 120 psi) and then automatically shuts off. A predetermined dip in pressure (usually around 80 to 90 psi) reactivates the cycle.

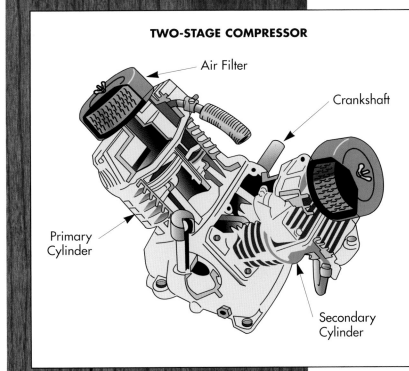

TWO-STAGE COMPRESSOR

Air Filter

Crankshaft

Primary Cylinder

Secondary Cylinder

COMPRESSOR FEATURES

Compressors are available in a wide variety of tank configurations. They can have no tank at all, a small pancake- or hot dog–style tank, twin tanks, or one large cylindrical tank.

No-tank

One tank configuration is no tank at all. Small oil-free compressors are available sans tank; but they run continuously and are hard-pressed to deliver the kind of air volume you'll need (*top photo*). They're best suited for light jobs like inflating pool toys and sports equipment and for powering low-cfm tools like an airbrush. Without a tank for storage, such a compressor runs continuously; so any air tool you hook up must be of the "bleeder" variety—that is, it safely shunts off any air that it doesn't need to operate.

Small and medium tanks

Small and medium-sized tanks are available in two common setups: pancake or twin tank. Small tanks, like the pancake version shown in the middle photo, typically hold 1 to 4 gallons. Medium-sized tanks often consist of "twin" tanks; the tanks can be stacked vertically or horizontally. Medium tanks hold anywhere from 4 to 12 gallons. I prefer twin tanks for portables because you can carry the compressor with the tanks against your leg. Since a compressor gets hot with use, carrying it like this can prevent accidental burns.

One large tank

The larger the tank, the longer you can work at a desired pressure and flow rate—but at the cost of portability. Large compressors have a single tank that stores 10 to 60 gallons (*bottom photo*). One reasons many large compressors use a single tank is for balance. A single tank centered on the compressor helps make these very heavy tools easier to move around. A word of caution: The size of the tank does not reflect the ability of the compressor to produce high cfm.

Weight

What is "portable?" When I was in the Navy, the general rule was "paint it gray and put a handle on it." To this day, my back shudders at the thought of some of the "portable" gear I lugged around. To me, weight is a big deal. Even if wheels are involved, you still have to overcome gravity (*top photo*). If you're looking for a truly portable compressor, go to a home center or tool warehouse and pick up each portable and walk around the store. You'll quickly find out which style works best for you. Another misconception regarding portability is that if it has wheels, it must be portable. True, wheels make even a heavy compressor easier to move around—but they must be of proper size and located correctly. As to size, the bigger the better. Larger-diameter wheels will navigate steps and most obstructions with ease.

Balance

Even with reasonable weight and a good set of wheels, not all portable compressors are easy to maneuver. This has to do with the balance of the compressor itself, along with the number of wheels. It's nerve-racking to roll a single-wheel compressor up a ramp into a truck (*middle photo*). A dual-wheel compressor with wheels spread comfortably apart would be better. If you do decide to go with a single-wheel compressor, make sure to give it a spin in the parking lot to test its balance.

Tank location

The location of the tank or tanks on a portable compressor will also impact how easy it is to move around (*bottom photo*). This is especially true for small compressors without wheels. Pancake-style compressors typically have the tank centered below the engine for good balance. Twin-tank designs with tanks that are stacked vertically have pluses and minuses. With lighter tanks on one side, the compressor will tip when you pick it up. On the plus side, you can carry it with the tanks against your leg and prevent burns from a hot compressor.

Although compressors are rated by horsepower, what's really important is the *volume* of air they can produce at a sustained pressure. The secret to selecting a compressor is defining what tools you'll be using now and in the future. When you find a compressor that can produce the air you need, horsepower is insignificant.

Most air tools run at 90 psi (pounds per square inch)—a pressure that virtually every compressor is capable of producing. The catch is, what volume of air (at 90 psi) does the tool need to operate smoothly and efficiently? (Volume of airflow is measured in cfm, or cubic feet per minute.) All air tools have varying cfm needs; *see the cfm chart at right*. For instance, a narrow crown stapler used intermittently will need only 1 to 3 cfm. On the other hand, a random-orbit sander when run continuously will gulp 6 to 10 cubic feet of air per minute.

Since compressors are rated for a 50% duty cycle (half on/half off), running a tool continuously will make the compressor run more often—possibly continuously. To get around this, you'll need a compressor that produces a cfm higher than the highest-rated tool you're planning on using. Although it may sound like a good idea when a compressor salesman suggests doubling the highest cfm–rated tool you're planning on using to identify the maximum cfm rating for your dream compressor, it's not. Compressors capable of producing high cfm require 220 volts to operate—which may not be readily accessible in your shop or home.

TYPICAL CFM PRODUCTION

Compressor Type	CFM at 90 psi
Tankless	1–2
Hand-carried	2–4
Medium-duty	3–5
Heavy-duty	5–10

TYPICAL CFM REQUIREMENTS OF AIR TOOLS

Tool	cfm	psi
3/8" drill	4–6	70–90
3/8" impact wrench	3–6	70–90
Stapler	1–3	70–90
Brad nailer	2–4	70–90
Finish nailer	4–7	70–90
Framing nailer	4–10	70–90
Coil nailer	5–9	70–90
Pressure washer	3–5	70–90
Sandblast gun	2–3	30–90
Random-orbit sander	6–10	70–90
Jitterbug sander	5–9	70–90
In-line sander	5–9	70–90
Screwdriver	2–6	70–90
Air brush	1–2	25–40
Paint sprayer	1–5	10–70

COMPRESSOR RECOMMENDATIONS

▪ If you're planning on using high-cfm tools like framing nailers and random-orbit sanders, I recommend a large compressor (around 3 hp) with a 20- to 30-gallon tank. These will cost anywhere from $400 to $800, depending on quality.

If you won't be working with air-gobbling tools, a small portable compressor (around 1½ hp)

with a 4- to 6-gallon tank and a 25-foot hose will do the job. Here again, depending on quality, they'll set you back between $200 and $400.

Regardless of the size, I recommend sticking with an oil-lubricated compressor. If properly maintained, it'll last a lot longer than an oil-less compressor. I also like the fact that if it breaks down, I can tear it apart and fix it. Quite often, when an oil-less compressor goes down, it's not repairable (or if it is, it'd cost less to buy a new one).

SETTING UP A SYSTEM

Your first task with a new compressor is setting up the system. If it's an oil-lubricated compressor, begin by adding quality compressor oil according to the manufacturer's instructions. Remove the dipstick and fill the crankcase with oil to the upper or full oil level mark—make sure the compressor is level for this. Note: Multi-viscosity oils are not recommended for air compressors. Oil-less compressors are ready to go right out of the box.

Before you plug in either variety, make sure that the pressure switch is off and that the air outlet of the compressor is connected to an air hose that's terminated with either a quick-connect fitting with an automatic shutoff or an air tool. Turn the pressure switch on and adjust the regulator to the desired pressure. Once the tank fills to the set pressure, the compressor should automatically turn off (unless it's a continuous-running tankless compressor).

Portable

The advantage of a portable compressor setup is that your compressor will be ready to go at all times. Just carry or wheel it to the job site. Instead of getting tangled in the air hose, I suggest building or buying a hose caddy or reel that attaches to the compressor (*top photo*).

Permanent

Installing a compressor in a more permanent location doesn't mean it has to lose its portability. With the judicious placement of a couple of quick-connect fittings, you can unhook the compressor and roll it away. Simple installs like the one shown in the bottom photo feature a wall-mounted regulator assembly and hose reel. More-permanent installations use copper pipe to extend air lines around the shop. This allows you to create separate lines for tools that require lubrication (like drills and impact wrenches) and for spraying equipment, where the air must be oil-free to prevent contaminating the finish.

It's also a good idea to install a shutoff valve, such as a gate valve, between the compressor and the filter/regulator assembly in case you want to be able to disconnect the air hose without first emptying the compressor's tank. Two additional things here. First, make sure to slope the piping down toward the compressor to help condensation moisture drain safely away. Second, install petcocks or valves at the low points, and drain them whenever you drain the moisture out of your compressor.

Some of the first accessories you should purchase for your compressor are designed to enhance the performance of your air tools—and protect them from damage. In particular, a regulator, a lubricator, and a filter. In many cases, you can buy these as an assembled set.

Regulators

A regulator is installed between a compressor and an air tool to control the pressure to the tool. Most models have a built-in gauge to monitor outgoing pressure and provide a regulated output from 0 to 150 psi (*top photo*). Regulators are rated by maximum pressure (psi) and maximum airflow (cfm). Some compressors have a built-in regulator, but these are often cheaply made and inaccessible. For permanent installations, it's worth the cost to install a separate regulator. It'll last longer and be easier to adjust, and you can mount it in a convenient location.

Filters

An in-line filter is a must on any compressed-air system (*middle photo*). Contaminants in the form of oil, water, and dirt will otherwise flow unchecked to your air tools. This can cause a horde of problems. First, the inevitable water that results from compressing air will harm any tool you use. To prevent your tools from rusting from the inside out, it's imperative that the water be removed. Dirt from a compressor or the air lines is also bad for your tools. Small bits of metal or rust can clog up an intake port, thereby reducing pressure and efficiency.

Lubricators

A lubricator (or oiler) is placed between a compressor and the air line to periodically inject tiny droplets of oil into the line (*bottom photo*). This is good since most air tools require periodic lubrication, and a self-dispensing oil lubricator will make your air tools virtually maintenance-free. CAUTION: If you plan to use a spray gun, do not install a lubricator on the main line. If you want to use a lubricator and a spray gun, install a separate line and use a hose that's dedicated to spraying. If you don't, oil will mix with and contaminate the finish.

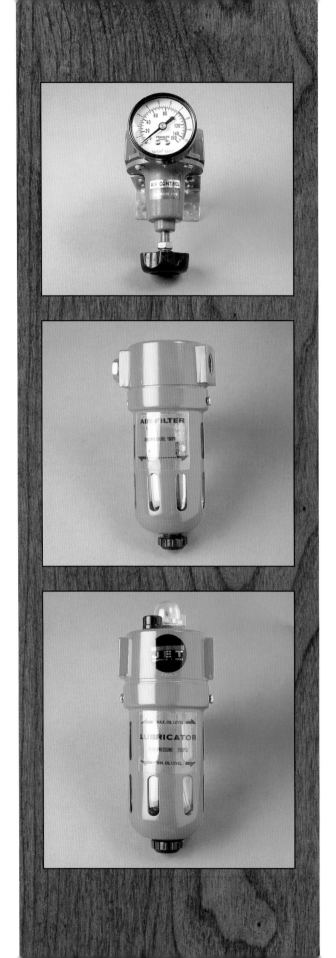

HOSES AND FITTINGS

Standard and lightweight hose

Most standard air hose is made of PVC and is rated to handle from 150 to 300 psi. Relatively inexpensive, PVC hose resists lubricating oils and sunlight, and remains flexible over a wide range of temperatures (*top photo*). All come with threaded fittings (either $1/4$" or $3/8$" NPT threads). Quality hoses are made of neoprene rubber and are reinforced with braided polyester; they're considerably more expensive, but they last longer.

Popular in the construction trades, clear plastic hose is rugged yet lightweight (*top inset*). The weight of a hose may not seem like much, but after lugging a heavy hose around all day, you'll be dreaming of ways to pare down the weight. A lightweight hose will help considerably, but not without exacting a price. This type of hose isn't as flexible as standard hose and has an annoying habit of not lying flat—it often gets tangled around your feet.

Recoil hose

Retractable recoil hose is standard in shops and plants around the world (*middle photo*). Quite often it's attached to an air line running along the ceiling. Grab it and pull it down when you need it. It recoils up out of the way when you're done. Most have swivel-type fittings with spring guards to help prevent kinks in the hose.

Fittings

The most common type of fitting used for air hose and tools is the brass threaded fitting (*bottom inset*). This is a screw-type fitting that's tightened with a wrench. Quick-connect fittings, on the other hand, let you connect and disconnect tools from the air line without having to shut down the compressor (*bottom photo*). That's because the female half of the coupling has a built-in shutoff valve.

AIR NAILERS

I know I shouldn't admit this, but I can't hammer a nail for beans. It's a good thing I'm a woodworker, not a carpenter—I rarely use metal fasteners at all, and when I do it's a screw. But I do use nails for construction, and I've found that I'm using finish nails and brads more now, with the added precision that most air guns offer.

Framing nailer

When I first saw a framing nailer in use, I knew I had to have one. I was visiting a finish carpenter friend at a construction site, and I noticed a fellow toenailing studs in a wall. If you've ever tried this, you know how difficult it is to hold a stud in perfect position as you nail it in place; every time you hit the nail, the stud moves—very frustrating. When I saw the carpenter toenail with a framing nailer, the stud didn't move at all—and the nail was set in the perfect amount. That's because a framing nailer literally shoots the nail into the wood in one quick motion (*top photo*).

Finish nailers

If you're not interested in framing and construction but often do trim or finish work, a finish nailer will make the job a whole lot easier. Not as beefy as a framing nailer, a finish nailer shoots 15- and 16-gauge nails varying in length from $3/4$" to $2^3/4$". This makes them ideal for attaching trim, chair railing (*middle photo*), crown molding, window and door casings, and so forth. A professional model can easily cost $400, while a less expensive imported version can be purchased for less than half that.

When looking to buy a finish nailer, the first choice you need to make is what gauge nail to shoot. Thinner, 16-gauge nails are less likely to split wood than the heavier 15-gauge. But the disadvantage to the smaller gauge is that the nails tend to follow the grain in wood and often deflect off course, sometimes protruding out the face.

Additional features to look for are

FASTENER SELECTION CHART

Fastener Type	Application	Size
Staples	upholstery	22 gauge, $3/16$"–$9/16$"
	case construction	19 gauge, $1/4$"–1"
	roof sheathing	16 gauge 1"–2"
	subflooring	15 gauge, $1^1/2$"–$2^1/2$"
Roundhead nails	framing	12d–16d, 2"–$3^1/4$"
	decking	12d–16d, 2"–$3^1/4$"
	wall sheathing	12d–16d, $2^1/4$"–3"
	fencing	8d–12d, $1^3/4$"–$2^3/4$"
Finish nails	furniture work	16 gauge, 1"–2"
	cabinet assembly	15 gauge, $1^1/4$"–$2^1/2$"
	trim	15 gauge, $1^1/4$"–$2^1/2$"
Brads	paneling	20 gauge, $5/8$"–1"
	light trim	20 gauge, 1"–$1^9/16$"
	light assembly	20 gauge, 1"–$1^9/16$"

whether the magazine is straight or angled (*see the sidebar below*), and how the fasteners load into the magazine. While a typical framing nailer requires 4 to 6 cfm at 90 psi, a finish nailer can get by with around half that.

Narrow crown staplers

Narrow crown staplers are gaining rapidly in popularity among homeowners, especially those who enjoy working with wood (*top photo*). The most common staplers shoot $1/4$" or $3/8$" staples in gauges ranging from 16 to 22. They require only 1 to 2 cfm at 90 psi and so can be used with smaller compressors. The major drawback to using a staple is its footprint. As it's difficult to hide the head of a staple, they're primarily used in areas that won't be seen.

Brad nailers

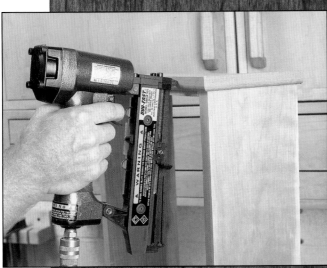

Of all the air guns out there, I use my brad nailer more often than all the others combined (*middle photo*). That's because a brad nailer is so versatile—it can tack on molding strips, affix drawer bottoms, quickly assemble jigs and fixtures, just about anything. Brad nailers typically shoot 18-gauge brads that can vary in length from $5/8$" to $1\,1/2$". One feature I really like about most brad nailers is that they can shoot brads of varying length. Just pick the right length for the job, and load it in the magazine.

ANGLED AND STRAIGHT MAGAZINES

As a general rule of thumb, 15-gauge nailers (*left in bottom photo*) have angled magazines, while 16-gauge nailers come with straight magazines (*right in bottom photo*). You can, however, find both 15- and 16-gauge nailers with either straight or angled magazines. I prefer an angled magazine since it lets me get into corners and other tight spots that a straight magazine can't navigate, such as applying crown molding around the ceiling perimeter of a room.

AIR NAILER SAFETY

Just like any other power tool, an air nailer can be dangerous, even fatal, if used improperly. The secret to preventing accidents is learning and following the safety rules for the tool. I'm sure that some of the safety precautions I'll discuss here will seem like common sense. But the number of air nailer accidents that continue to happen on a daily basis indicates that common sense is being ignored.

If you start practicing safe tool handling and nailing technique now, it'll quickly develop into habit. And the few extra seconds these take can save you or someone else a serious injury. Make sure to take the time to read and follow the safety precautions described in the user's manual. It's also a good idea to check the safety mechanism of the nailer on a regular basis; if it doesn't work properly, take it in to a service center immediately for repair.

Wear glasses

The number one safety rule for using an air nailer is to wear safety glasses—every time you pick up a gun, get in the habit of checking to make sure you've got them on (*top photo*). Most manufacturers include a pair with the air nailer. Since air nailers often cause fragments or fasteners to ricochet at odd angles, anyone working in your immediate area should also have safety glasses on. Safety glasses not only protect your eyes from fragments, but also protect them from the burst of air or exhaust from the nailer.

Hose clearance

Air hoses often cause accidents. First off, if the hose gets tangled around your feet, you can trip and fall (*bottom photo*). Second, if you're carrying an air nailer when you trip, you'll

damage the nailer, or more importantly, you could accidentally fire a fastener into something or someone (including yourself). The simplest way to prevent this is to be aware of the hose at all times; keep excess hose coiled away from your feet. Some types of hose, like the plastic one shown here, have a tendency to not lie flat. Be especially careful when working with these.

Always disconnect before servicing

If there's one safety rule that I constantly see being ignored, it's loading a magazine or clearing a jam without first disconnecting the air hose. This is like trying to clean a handgun while it's loaded—it's just a matter of time before someone gets hurt. Disconnecting the hose takes one, maybe two seconds (*top photo*). Take the time to do this—you'll be glad you did. WARNING: Because it's self-sealing, never install a female quick-connect on a nailer—the gun can remain pressurized even after you've disconnected the hose.

Don't carry with trigger depressed

Probably the number one cause of serious nailer injuries is carrying a nailer set up for "bounce" firing with the trigger depressed. As long as the trigger is depressed, the nailer will shoot a fastener whenever the safety mechanism or contact point is depressed. The nailer can't tell the difference between a 2×4 and your knee. Again, I'm sure this seems obvious, but I've caught myself doing it when laying roof shingles. To prevent this, don't just release the trigger, remove your finger completely, as shown in the middle photo.

Never point gun toward yourself

I can't tell you how many times I've seen someone point a nailer at themselves, as in the bottom photo. In every case when I've pointed out what they were doing, they stepped back, shook their head, and turned red. If you work with air nailers a lot, it's easy to become complacent. I often suggest to folks that they use the same mindset for handling an air nailer as they'd use for handling a weapon—although air nailers don't have the range of a handgun, they are just as dangerous.

USING AN AIR NAILER

Framing nailers

Without a doubt, the ability to toenail a stud in perfect position with the pull of a trigger is what sold me on framing nailers. Holding the gun at the proper angle, press the nosepiece firmly into the workpiece until the spiked tip grabs hold, and then continue pressing to engage the safety mechanism. Pull the trigger to drive the nail (*top photo*). Since a nailer drives the nail in the blink of an eye, you'll find you don't have to have a death grip on the workpiece.

Finish nailers

In many situations where you're using a finish nailer, you're pressing a part against a wall or ceiling or you're pressing two parts together. When working against a wall or ceiling that's not plumb or level, insert shims as needed to support the part; when pressing two parts together, support them on a stout table or workbench. Also, the tip you use with a finish nailer will have a lot to do with how well it works. I've had best luck with a rubber tip (*middle photo*). Larger cushion tips are available, but they're usually round, and they don't fit into crevices well like the small, rectangular rubber ones.

Narrow crown staplers

When it comes to using a narrow crown stapler, one thing that's different from other nailers is the precautions you have to take because of the size of the staple. Since staples can be much larger than brads, or finish nails, you have to be careful where you shoot them, as they have a tendency to split wood (*see below*). The other thing with a stapler is, since it's driving two points instead of one, it often requires greater cfm than a finish nailer or brad nailer.

Lighter-gauge staples have a tendency to follow the grain when shot into hardwood. As the point of the staple drives into the wood, it is easily deflected when it hits a growth ring.

When this happens, the staple takes the path of least resistance and, depending on the workpiece, can even shoot out of the side (*bottom drawing*). Following the grain also leads to splitting. This is especially true near the edge of a workpiece. Here again, orienting the staple perpendicular to the grain can help.

SPRAY GUNS

If you've ever spent all weekend applying numerous coats of finish to a large project, it should come as no surprise to find that spray guns are one of the most popular accessories for a compressor. Spray guns are capable of atomizing a lot more than paint: You can spray stains and dyes, clear finishes (like varnish, shellac, and lacquer), even adhesives like contact cement (this is how most cabinet manufacturers apply adhesive).

Spray guns come in many types and styles. Two of the most common types are shown in the top photo: a standard siphon-feed gun for general-purpose spraying (*left in photo*), and a detail sprayer for fine work and touch-up jobs (*right in photo*). The first step in selecting a spray gun is to determine what type of materials you'll likely be spraying. Lightweight materials like stain can be sprayed successfully with a relatively inexpensive gun. Heavier materials like varnish and paint require a higher-quality gun.

A high-quality gun (costing $100 to $300) will offer a wide variety of fluid tips and air caps (*bottom drawing*) that can be used in different combinations to spray almost anything. Spraying heavier materials also requires a heavy-duty compressor—one capable of producing up to 15 to 20 cfm. Check with the manufacturer of the spray gun to see whether the gun you have in mind is capable of spraying the materials you want—most reputable manufacturers have charts available that list the correct fluid tip/air cap combination for specific materials.

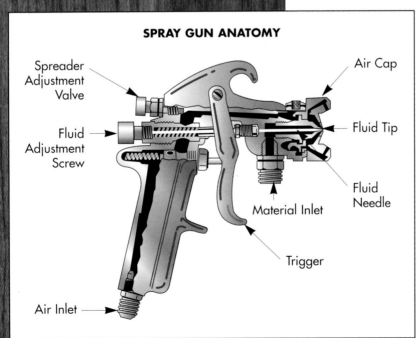

SPRAY GUN ANATOMY

Spreader Adjustment Valve

Fluid Adjustment Screw

Air Inlet

Air Cap

Fluid Tip

Fluid Needle

Material Inlet

Trigger

SPRAY-PAINTING

The first thing you should know about spraying on paint or finish is that the time devoted to actually spraying can be a small portion of the overall job. The bulk of your time will be devoted to preparing to spray and then cleaning up afterwards.

Prepare the surface to be sprayed

Before you even open a can of paint or finish, you'll need to prepare the surface to be sprayed. Start by removing all dust, dirt, or loose particles. If you're spraying in the same room where you've built the project, let the dust settle and then vacuum the project and work area thoroughly. Use tape to mask off areas as needed (*top photo*).

Prepare the spray area

Regardless of the finish you're applying, spraying always generates a fine mist. To prevent this from covering your shop and coating your lungs, you need to set up an appropriate area to spray. If the object you're spraying is small, you can set up a simple spray booth with a scrap of plywood on a pair of sawhorses. A pre-folded "science fair" display board (available at office supply stores) works great for a temporary backdrop. Covering an ordinary floor fan with a filter will help draw the finish away from you and your shop (*middle photo*).

Check viscosity of the finish

Although many finishes can be sprayed right from the can, there are times when you'll need to thin the finish in order to get a smooth, even finish. Most manufacturers provide thinning recommendations right on the can. Some spray gun manufacturers will indicate how thin a material should be for a specific needle/tip combination. You can measure the thickness of a material, or "viscosity," with a viscosity cup (*bottom photo*). Timing how long it takes for the material to drain from the cup indicates its viscosity and whether it needs to be thinned or not.

Strain finish and fill the canister

Cleanliness is extremely important in spraying, since even the smallest particle of dust or dirt can ruin a job. You've cleaned the work area and project, but how about the finish? Even if you've just opened a fresh can, odds are that there are impurities in it; cans that have been previously opened will undoubtedly have collected dust and dirt. To prevent impurities from affecting your finish, take the time to strain the material before filling the spray canister (*inset photo*). A disposable paper filter like the one shown here (*top left photo*) makes this a quick and easy task. When you're spraying only a small amount, you can combine straining and filling by inserting the strainer into the canister and then filling.

Spray a test pattern

Once the canister is filled, attach the air hose and adjust the compressor pressure according to the spray gun manufacturer's directions to match the type of finish you're spraying. Then, holding the gun about 8" to 12" away from a scrap of cardboard or plywood, give the trigger a quick pull to spray a test pattern (*middle photo*). If the material sputters, odds are it's too thick and needs to be thinned.

Basic technique

If you've never sprayed before, take some time to practice correct spraying technique. Start by holding the gun 8" to 12" from the surface. Depress the trigger, and begin the stroke. Keep the gun moving in a straight line, parallel to and an even distance away from the surface (*bottom drawing*). Make sure the tip of the gun is also parallel to the surface. A common mistake is to move the gun in an arc, as shown; doing so will lay down an uneven pattern—too much material in the center and not enough at the edges.

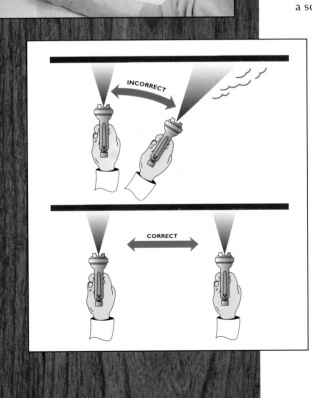

Adjust gun for desired pattern

On most spray guns, there are two controls that need adjusting to create a solid, even pattern. Start by adjusting the fluid control to get good material flow (*top photo*). Then adjust the pressure of the fluid as it flows to the tip by adjusting the air-control knob. Getting the proper material flow can be tricky and will likely require some trial and error. But as long as the material viscosity and incoming air pressure are correct, this shouldn't take long.

Overlap strokes

To reduce the likelihood of thin spots and to guarantee even coverage, each pass that you make with the spray gun should overlap the previous stroke by about half (*middle photo*). On large, flat surfaces, like table tops or walls, you'll achieve more consistent coverage by making two lighter passes in opposite directions than by making a single heavy pass.

Don't tilt the gun

Just as moving the spray gun in an arc will create an uneven pattern, tilting the spray gun at an angle will also cause problems. When the tip of the gun is not parallel to the work surface, the material being sprayed will lay down heavier on either the top or the bottom, depending on which way the gun is tilted (*bottom drawing*). This often results in sagging or runs. If you're having problems keeping the gun level, consider attaching a small bubble level to the gun as a visual reference.

Setup and follow-through

Just as with a good golf or baseball swing, setup and follow-through are important parts of good spraying technique. To get the most consistent results, start your stroke 6" to 8" in front of the surface. Depress the trigger and move the gun steadily across the surface. When you reach the end of the surface, don't stop. Instead, continue moving and spraying for another 6" to 8" past the edge.

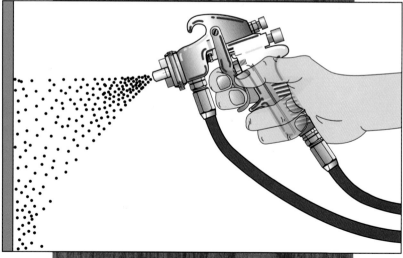

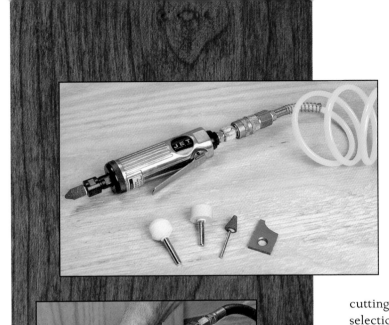

USING AIR TOOLS

Die grinders

Although die grinders have been used in industry for years, they're rapidly being used more and more in home workshops (*top photo*). Their aggressive abrasive action will quickly remove even the most stubborn rust. They're also handy for sharpening cutting tools. Most die grinders come with a selection of abrasive wheels and "points" that slip into either a $1/8$" or $1/4$" collet. Smaller die grinders require 3 to 6 cfm at 90 psi, while the heavy-duty or "industrial" versions need upwards of 12 cfm.

Drills

Since air-powered tools don't require a separate motor, they're smaller than their electric counterparts (*middle photo*). That's one of the biggest advantages to an air drill—the smaller size lets you get into corners and hard-to-reach places that an electric drill just can't handle. Their compact size also makes it easy to "get behind" the drill and efficiently transfer your body weight to the drill for those heavy-duty boring jobs. A typical air drill requires around 4 cfm at 90 psi. They're also available with variable speed and keyless chucks.

Screwdrivers

Just like an air-powered drill, a pneumatic screwdriver is smaller than its electric counterpart, but just as powerful (*bottom photo*). Here again, this makes it ideal for cramped spaces. As with an electric driver, most air screwdrivers come with an adjustable clutch that allows you to drive a screw flush with a surface without stripping or breaking the screw. Many air-powered screwdrivers also have quick-change chucks that accept standard $1/4$" hex bits. Typical air consumption for an air screwdriver is 4 cfm at 90 psi.

AIR-POWERED SANDERS

Air-powered sanders are becoming more and more popular in workshops because they're lighter, quieter, and in many cases more powerful than their electric counterparts. Common air-powered sanding tools are: random-orbit sanders (commonly referred to as dual-action sanders, in the automotive trades), jitterbug (or orbital) sanders, and in-line (or finish) sanders. The only disadvantage I've found to air-powered sanders is that they're air hogs. Virtually every type gobbles up air. This means you'll need a stout compressor to run them—a unit that's capable of producing 4 to 6 cfm. You can run these on a smaller compressor, but it'll run constantly.

Random-orbit sanders

Of all the air sanders out there, the random-orbit is my favorite (*top photo*). Its unique sanding pattern lets you sand wood with almost total disregard to grain. Because of this, they're terrific for leveling joints where the grain of the parts is perpendicular (like a frame-and-panel door). Note: Always start a random-orbit sander with the disk in contact with the surface; doing otherwise can cause swirl marks.

Jitterbug sanders

For years, jitterbug sanders were the main-stay in woodworking. They're reliable, leave few swirl marks, and are inexpensive (*middle photo*). Although I do reach for a random-orbit sander for most sanding jobs, a jitterbug offers a number of advantages. Because it's not as aggressive as a random-orbit, it's easier to use in confined spaces, and its square pad allows you to reach into corners (like inside a drawer, or all the way into the back of a shelf). Their less-aggressive action also makes them ideal for delicate jobs where finesse is required.

In-line sanders

An in-line sander uses a back-and-forth motion that most approximates hand sanding.

The big difference is that the stroke is only about $1/2$". In-line sanders (often referred to as straight-line sanders) use long strips of sandpaper that are held in place with built-in clamps (*bottom photo*). Although not as aggressive as random-orbit sanders, these tools provide the ultimate in smooth, flat surfaces.

Compressor Maintenance

Daily

One of the best compressor maintenance habits you can develop takes only a few seconds—a quick visual check of the overall condition of the compressor. Also, nothing will more seriously shorten the life of an oil-lubricated compressor quicker than running it when it's low on oil. If you really want to extend the life of your compressor, check the oil level before each use (*top photo*). Unlike a car, where it's best to check the oil when the motor is warm, you can check the oil in a compressor when it's cold.

Weekly

When air is compressed, moisture in the air condenses to form liquid water. If you don't remove this water from the tanks, it can lead to rust and eventual rupture. All compressor manufacturers install petcocks or drains on the underside of the tank(s) so you can prevent this from happening. After you've shut your compressor down for the day, loosen the petcock to allow pressurized air in the tank to blow out any water (*middle photo*). After 5 or 10 seconds, close the petcock.

Monthly

Just like the water heater in your home, every compressor should have a pressure-relief valve that will open to drain off excessive pressure that has built up in a tank. On a monthly basis, you should check the operation of this. Most valves have a pull on the valve to make this easy (*bottom photo*). With the tank filled with air, pull on the valve to make sure air can escape; if it doesn't, the valve is faulty and should replaced immediately.

Also, since a compressor needs a constant supply of fresh air, it's important to keep the air filter clean (*bottom inset*). If it clogs, compressor efficiency will drop as it struggles to pull in air.

MAINTAINING AIR NAILERS

Most air nailers require both internal and external lubrication to run smoothly. Internal lubrication can be accomplished by three methods: with a lubricator that's built into the system, with a small in-line oiler that's attached directly to the fastening tool, or by injecting oil to the intake of the tool before use. (Note: Adding oil to the intake is generally seen as a supplement to one of the automatic lubricators mentioned above, not as a replacement.)

Before using any of these methods of internal lubrication, check your owner's manual to make sure your nailer requires it. Some manufacturers have introduced "oil-free" or "permanently oiled" nailers that require no internal lubrication. Injecting oil into these nailers will actually cause damage.

Regardless of whether your nailer requires internal lubrication, all fastening tools will work better and last longer if the external moving parts and linkages receive periodic lubrication. Here again, check the owner's manual to see what the manufacturer recommends.

Feed in-line

If you don't have a lubricator built into your air system that automatically injects oil into the air line, the next closest thing is an in-line oiler (*top photo*). They attach directly to a gun and accept a standard air hose. Since they hold much less oil than a full-sized lubricator, you have to keep an eye on the oil level. These are particularly useful for larger guns like framing or coil nailers that drive big fasteners.

Lubrication points

In addition to keeping the internal parts of the nailer well-lubricated, there are numerous external linkages and moving parts that will benefit from periodic attention (*bottom drawing*)—in particular, the magazine mechanism, the nosepiece area and associated safety linkages, and the trigger area. Consult your owner's manual for recommended lubricant and lubrication points, and for how often it should be applied.

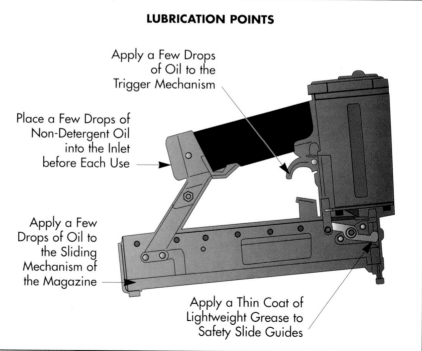

LUBRICATION POINTS

Apply a Few Drops of Oil to the Trigger Mechanism

Place a Few Drops of Non-Detergent Oil into the Inlet before Each Use

Apply a Few Drops of Oil to the Sliding Mechanism of the Magazine

Apply a Thin Coat of Lightweight Grease to Safety Slide Guides

Inject oil in air intake

Another option for keeping the interior parts of an air nailer running smoothly is to simply inject some oil into the nailer manually (*top photo*). How much and how often you inject oil depends on the gun and the type of work you're doing. If you're using a brad nailer to fasten parts together, a couple of drops at the beginning of the job will do. If you're using a coil nailer to install roofing shingles, it's best to add oil every time you refill the magazine.

Oil linkages

Before you apply any lubricant, check your owner's manual to see what the manufacturer recommends (typically it's S.A.E. no. 20-weight). Virtually all manufacturers will warn you to steer clear of detergent oils. Regular air tool oil will do, but it's often very light and won't last long. I like to apply oil or a thin coating of lightweight grease to the lubrication points and then wipe off any excess with a clean rag right before I put a nailer back in its case (*middle photo*). If it has been in storage for a while, I'll lubricate it before using it again.

O-RINGS

Most nailers use O-rings internally to create a seal around the piston as it moves up and down to drive in fasteners. These O-rings periodically require lubrication and will occasionally need to be replaced. To do this, gently pull off the cap. There's usually an O-ring on the underside of the cap, which maintains the seal on the cylinder. If you've purchased a rebuild kit, replace each O-ring in turn as you continue to disassemble the gun. Keep the old and new O-rings separate to prevent mixing them up. As you replace each O-ring, apply a generous amount of O-ring grease or ordinary petroleum jelly to each O-ring (*photo at right*). When done, reverse the steps you took to disassemble the nailer to put it back together.

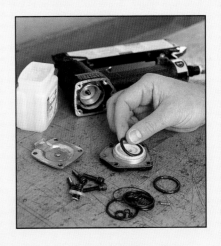

Photo courtesy of Record Tools, copyright 2001

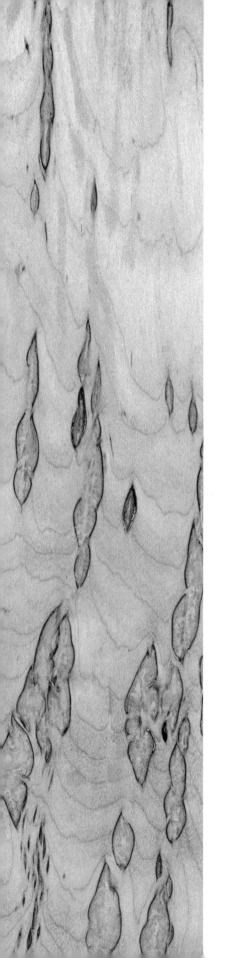

LATHES

When Chris, my photographer, starting taking the photos for this chapter, he was mesmerized by the lathe's spinning wood. After watching me for a while, Chris called a lathe "sort of a pottery wheel for wood." That's how I think of it, too.

I love turning, especially after completing a demanding project like a Morris chair. I chuck up a piece of wood and start making chips. I often let the wood show me the final shape, and I stop frequently to examine the grain as it changes under the gouge. This is about as free-form as it gets with wood. At the other extreme, the lathe excels at exacting work, like turning a hollow vessel or a set of matched table legs.

What's more, you can go from start to finish in anywhere from five minutes to an hour. Need a quick gift? A turned box, a wine stopper, a baby rattle can be made in less than an hour.

The lathe is one of the oldest woodworking tools: It's been used for centuries to shape wood. Whether you create decorative bowls or spindles for a chair back, you're part of a respected tradition that's as valued today as ever.

The Coronet Minor lathe shown at left went into production in the 1950s. The basic lathe was available with 18, 24, or 30 inches between centers, and a 9-inch turning capacity over the bed. Other attachments (saw table, mortiser) were also available to convert it into a combination machine.

TYPES OF LATHES

Like all the other power tools, there are numerous lathes on the market for you to choose from. Each of these can be classified as either a stationary, bench-top, or mini-lathe. The one you choose will depend on the type of work you plan to do (*see the sidebar on page 175 for lathe recommendations*).

Stationary

I don't know many woodworkers who can justify a large stationary lathe like the one shown in the top photo. Unless you're turning professionally, are independently wealthy, or just like large tools, there's little reason to buy a lathe this big. These beefy machines typically feature a stand, bed, and parts that are made from heavy cast iron. The motors are often 2-hp and larger, with variable speeds. These industrial-strength lathes often tip the scales at $^1/_4$ to $^1/_2$ ton. The price tag is also hefty—anywhere from $2,000 to $5,000.

Bench-top

In my opinion, a bench-top lathe is all the lathe that the average woodworker will need in the shop. Bench-top lathes can be mounted to a workbench or other stand, but many now come with a set of legs or a metal stand (*middle photo*). This type of lathe will usually come with a $^3/_4$-hp or 1-hp motor—plenty of power for most turning tasks. A bench-top lathe can be had for as little as $350, or you can pay over $1,000.

Mini-lathes

Mini-lathes are a relative newcomer to the lathe market and have become popularized by the latest turning trend—pens. These diminutive lathes really are bench-top lathes and are light enough that you can pick one up and store it away when not in use (*bottom photo*). Most have a $^1/_2$-hp motor, and although they can handle relatively large chucks of wood (the lathe shown here will accept a 7" × 14" blank), I recommend that you stick with small projects like pens, brackets, wine stoppers, and so forth.

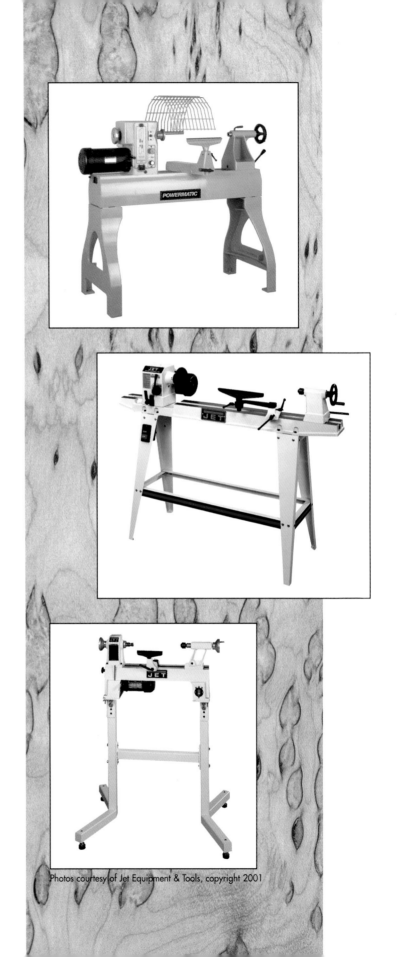

Photos courtesy of Jet Equipment & Tools, copyright 2001

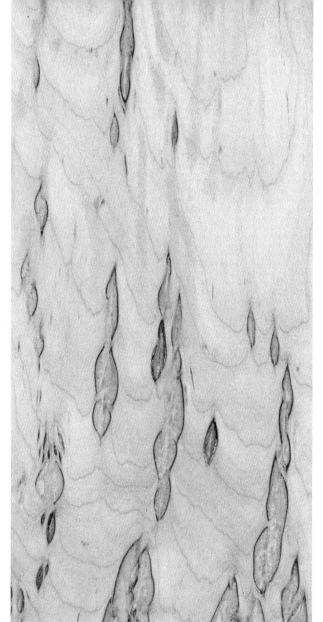

Regardless of the size, all lathes consist of four main components: a bed, a headstock and motor unit, a tailstock, and a tool rest (*bottom drawing*). The bed is the foundation of the lathe, and all the other parts attach to it, and most move back and forth on it (the headstock may be permanently attached to the bed). Although the bed is often overlooked, its rigidity will have a huge impact on lathe performance (*for more on bed styles, see page 174*).

The headstock typically houses the motor, which is usually connected to the main spindle via a drive belt. Stepped pulleys offer a range of speeds by changing the position of the belt. A tapered hole in the end of the spindle accepts the drive center—typically either a #1 or #2 Morse taper. The end of the spindle is usually threaded to accept lathe accessories, such as a faceplate, screw chuck, or scroll chuck. On some lathes, the headstock pivots so that you can turn "outboard" with the aid of an external tool rest.

The tailstock slides back and forth on the bed and supports the other end of the workpiece. Here again, the spindle has a tapered hole to accept a center. A large handwheel or knob on the tailstock allows you to easily move the center in or out to firmly support the workpiece. One or more tool rests also slide along the bed, and these are used to support the lathe tool during a cut. The tool rest can be adjusted up and down, at angles, and back and forth.

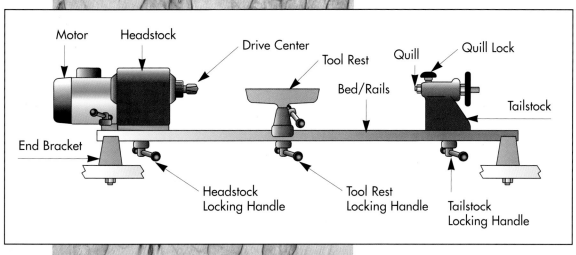

LATHE FEATURES

Besides the horsepower rating of a lathe, the two most common specs you'll want to check out are working capacities—particularly the bed length, or "working distance between centers," and the bed depth, or "swing over tool rest." These will tell you the maximum size workpiece that the lathe can safely handle.

Bed length and depth

Bed length, or working distance between centers, defines the distance between the headstock center and the tailstock center (*top photo*). Note that some manufacturers of smaller lathes offer extensions for their lathes, but these are never as rigid as a one-piece unit. Bed depth, or swing over tool rest (also called swing over bed), can be a bit confusing. Technically, the bed depth is the distance between the drive center and the bed (*middle drawing*). But this number is rarely given. Instead manufacturers double this and call it one of the above names. To add to the confusion, some manufacturers create a notch in the bed (a recessed bed) to increase the swing (*middle drawing*). It's important to note that this increases the swing only at the notch—this is fine for turning platters and shallow bowls, but has no effect on spindle-turning capacity.

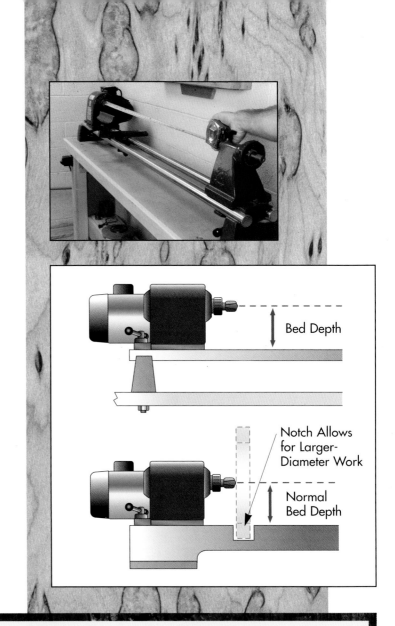

Bed Depth

Notch Allows for Larger-Diameter Work

Normal Bed Depth

TYPES OF LATHE BEDS

■ There are three common bed types, ranging from good to practically useless (*bottom drawing*). At the useless end of the scale are stamped metal beds. This type of bed does not offer either the weight or the rigidity that the headstock and tailstock need—the result is a machine that

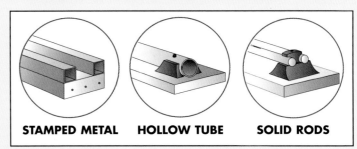

STAMPED METAL   HOLLOW TUBE   SOLID RODS

often vibrates so badly that turning is dangerous. Another weak system is a single hollow tube. Here again, it lacks both the weight and rigidity necessary. The best beds are made either with twin solid metal bars or from thick cast iron. Both are heavy and rigid and do a great job of dampening vibration.

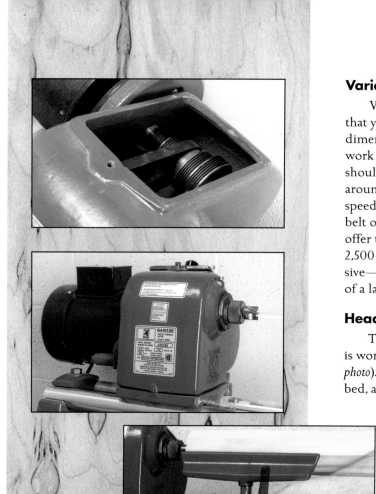

Variable speeds

Virtually all lathes offer varying speeds so that you can match the speed to both the dimensions of the workpiece and the type of work you're doing. At minimum, I think you should have at least five speeds, with the lowest around 350 rpm. On inexpensive lathes, the speeds are varied by changing the position of a belt on a step pulley (*top photo*). Deluxe lathes offer true variable speed, typically from 0 to 2,500 rpm; but be warned, this feature is expensive—it can easily add $250 to $500 to the cost of a lathe (but it sure is nice!).

Headstock

The headstock of a lathe you're considering is worthy of some serious attention (*middle photo*). Check to see how well it's secured to the bed, and whether it's designed to move or pivot (a nice feature). Stay away from spindles that are supported by ball bearings—they just don't hold up over time, and often introduce a huge amount of play. Better yet, look for a lathe that uses roller bearings. These long, cylindrical bearing are better suited to support the spindle while minimizing play. Also note that a #2 Morse taper is more common and that you'll find more accessories designed for this versus the #1.

Knobs

Although it might seem like a small detail, the types of knobs the lathe comes with (particularly on the tool rest) can be a blessing or a curse. Avoid (or consider replacing) knobs that aren't spring-loaded like the one shown in the bottom photo. Spring-loaded knobs allow you to push in the knob and spin it out of the way once the tool rest is locked in place. This is hugely important if you want to avoid constantly having to reposition the tool rest.

LATHE RECOMMENDATIONS

Unless you're a production turner, I'd recommend purchasing a quality bench-top lathe. Look for a cast-iron or solid-metal-bar bed, pivoting headstock with roller bearings, and at least five speeds. I'm on my third lathe now, and it's a Record CL-48—I love it. It's sturdy, is virtually vibration-free, and can handle spindles up to a whopping 48" in length. However, if you're looking only to turn small projects, a mini-lathe is a good choice. The only complaint I've heard from turners about these is that they often quickly exceed the lathe's capacities and wish they'd invested in a bench-top lathe from the start.

TOOL RESTS

The tool rest of a lathe allows you to present the lathe tool to the workpiece at the proper height and position. Since you'll use the tool rest for virtually every cut you make, it's important to know what makes a good one and what types are available. A quality tool rest will be made of cast iron with smooth, flat milled surfaces that contact the bed. The knob on the rest should be spring-loaded so that you can turn it out of the way once the rest is locked in place. There are three basic types of tool rests available: straight, bowl, and external.

Straight rests

Straight tools rests come in a variety of lengths and will be the rests you use most often (*top drawing*). An 8" to 10" rest is commonly included with most lathes, and you can purchase shorter 6" rests and longer 24" rests from most manufacturers. Rests longer than 12" typically have double shafts and will require an additional tool rest base for proper operation. Longer rests like this are worth their weight in gold when it comes to shaping long spindles: They allow you to make a continuous smooth cut instead of stopping frequently to reposition the rest.

Bowl rests

Specialized tool rests have been developed to help turners safely create bowls. They come in two flavors: right-angled (or 90-degree) and S-shaped (*middle drawing*). Both work well to better support a lathe tool inside the bowl. Without this type of rest, the lathe tool would extend out precariously past the rest and vibrate excessively, and would most likely catch and cause a nasty accident.

External rests

An external rest is used for "outboard" turning—that is, turning that's not done over the lathe bed. Some lathes offer outboard

capabilities by allowing you to attach a faceplate to the opposite end of the headstock, or else the headstock pivots to bring the drive center in front of the lathe or at its side. Since the tool rest that slides along the bed is no longer functional, here's where an external rest comes in (*bottom drawing*). This type of rest with splayed feet adjusts up and down so that you can continue turning. Some lathe manufacturers sell only the base because the head will accept your standard tool rests.

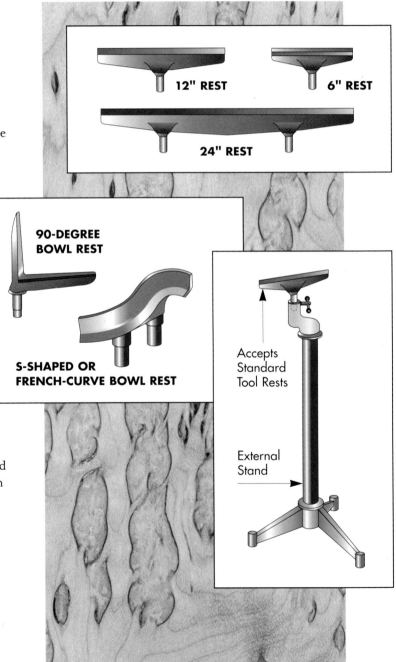

12" REST   6" REST

24" REST

90-DEGREE BOWL REST

S-SHAPED OR FRENCH-CURVE BOWL REST

Accepts Standard Tool Rests

External Stand

TURNING CENTERS

Turning centers are short, tapered metal rods that fit into the spindles of the headstock and tailstock. The headstock center is commonly referred to as a drive center and typically has two

or four spurs (I prefer four, as there's less tendency to split the workpiece) that are driven into the workpiece to grip it. When the motor is turned on, the center will "drive" the wood, spinning it at the selected speed. Tailstock centers support the wood and allow it to spin freely. They have either a cup center or a live center (*see below*). Regardless of the center type, the taper, called a Morse taper, is usually one of two sizes.

Morse tapers

The two tapers you'll find on most lathes are a #1MT (Morse taper) or a #2MT (*top and bottom, respectively, in the top photo*). By far, the #2MT is the most common. You may occasionally come across a #3MT, but these are fairly rare except on larger lathes. Please note that Morse taper adapters are available from most mail-order turning catalogs, but they're designed only to adapt smaller centers to fit machines with larger tapers.

Live centers

Unlike a cup center in a tailstock, where the workpiece rubs against the "rim" of the cup and will eventually burn, a live center uses a ball-bearing cap or cone that spins along with the workpiece (*middle photo*). I'm a real fan of this type of center, and the cup center that came with my lathe is off gathering dust somewhere. Once you use one of these, your old center will be collecting dust, too.

REMOVING STUBBORN CENTERS

Every now and then the tapered portions of a center do too good a job of gripping the tapered insides of the headstock or tailstock spindle. You can coerce the center out by tapping it with a scrap block and mallet, but this is not good for your spindle bearings. If your headstock or tailstock spindle is hollow, you can release a stubborn center by inserting a metal rod through the spindle and giving it a sharp rap with a hammer (*bottom drawing*). Many tailstocks are hollow to allow for deep hole boring (such as when making a lamp).

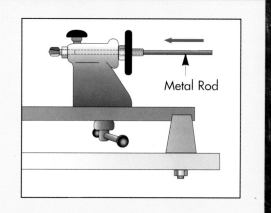

Metal Rod

LATHE TOOLS

Although there are a wide variety of turning tools available, they can all be broadly classified into one of four groups: gouges, chisels, scrapers, and specialty tools. For the most part, a turning tool consists of a metal blade or rod that's shaped for a specific task and fitted into a wood handle, usually via a tang with a ferrule to prevent the handle from splitting. Prices vary vastly, depending primarily on the quality and thickness of the tool steel. Quality lathe tools use premium high-speed steel (around Rockwell C60–C62) with thick, stiff blades.

Roughing gouge

A roughing gouge is a type of gouge that's designed for rough work—in particular, truing up a workpiece (taking it from square or octagonal to round). A roughing gouge can be identified by its square end (*top photo*). Leaving the end of the gouge square like this creates a sturdier edge, but limits the amount of close-in work you can do with it. I recommend a 1" roughing gouge—it's a good addition to any tool set.

Fingertip gouge

By far the most common type of gouge in use by most turners is the fingertip gouge, so named because its business end is shaped much like the tip of a finger (*middle photo*). The finger-shaped tip allows you to reach in and turn delicate details where other gouges can't go. Fingertip gouges are also commonly referred to a spindles gouges, as they're the main tool used to shape graceful curves on spindles. These gouges are commonly available in $^1/_4$", $^3/_8$", and $^1/_2$" sizes, with blade lengths averaging around 6".

Bowl gouge

Bowl gouges are similar to spindle or fingertip gouges except that they're usually made with stouter blades and longer handles (these tools are sometimes referred to as "long and strong" gouges). Blade lengths vary from 8" to 18", and handles can be anywhere from 14" to 24" in length (*bottom photo*). Both of these create a tool that's less susceptible to vibration and can be safely extended a bit farther past a tool rest. The $^1/_2$" bowl gouge is the favorite size of most bowl turners.

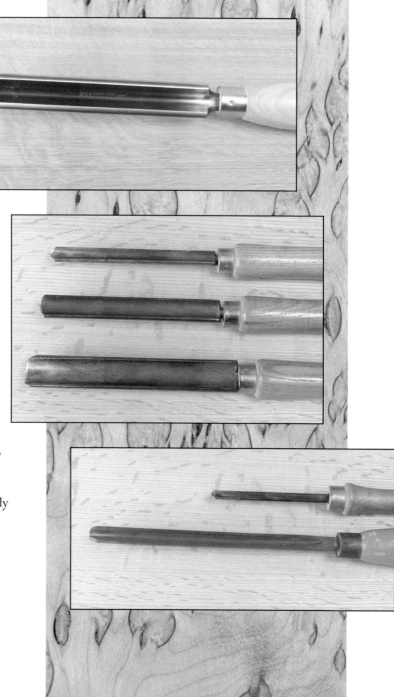

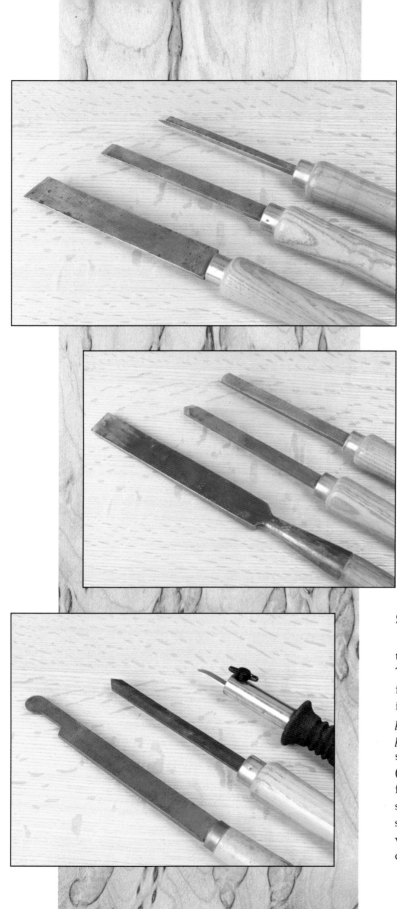

Skew chisel

Of all the lathe tools out there, the skew chisel has the worst reputation for being troublesome. And it is—when you first start turning. But with some practice, a chisel can be invaluable for smoothing cylinders, cutting-in details, and a variety of other tasks. The reason chisels can be troublesome is that it's very easy to "catch" the workpiece with the sharp ends. When this occurs, the chisel end digs into the workpiece and tears the wood. Proper technique will usually prevent this (*see page* 187 *for more on this*). Skew chisels come in sizes ranging from $1/4$" in width up to $1^1/4$" (*top photo*).

Scraper

Scrapers also have a not-so-glamorous reputation, but in my opinion it's undeserved. Scrapers are tools that cut wood with a scraping action instead of a cutting action (*middle photo*). They're made of flat stock, with the ends beveled in the desired shape. If you treat a lathe scraper the same way you'd treat a hand scraper—that is, you burnish an edge on it—the lathe scraper is also capable of producing whisper-thin shavings. Although some woodturners pooh-pooh scrapers, these tools are easy to use and are commonly used by world-class production turners.

Specialty tools

Any lathe tool that doesn't fit into one of the above classifications is a specialty tool. These can be gouges or scrapers that are modified for a specific task, such as truing up the interior of a bowl or turned box (*left in bottom photo*). Although the parting tool (*center in bottom photo*) is technically a scraper, it's usually sold as a specialty tool. Parting tools are used to "part off" (remove), or prepare to remove, a workpiece from the lathe. Other specialty tools include special hollowing tools for turning hollow vessels, and chatter tools (*right in bottom photo*), which vibrate intentionally to create stunning designs in the surface of a workpiece.

LATHE CHUCKS

A lathe chuck is any accessory for the lathe that's designed to grip a workpiece. Common versions include the screw chuck and the four-jaw chuck.

Screw chuck

A screw chuck is a hollow metal cap that threads onto the headstock spindle. A hole in the top center of the cap accepts a screw that passes through it and screws into the workpiece (*top photo*). This type of chuck is particularly useful for turning small items such as small lidded boxes. Since the workpiece is held in place only by the screw, it's a good idea to use the tailstock to support the other end while you true up the workpiece. ShopTip: You may find that inserting a strip or two of double-sided tape between the chuck and the workpiece will provide a superior grip and prevent the workpiece from spinning in case of a "catch."

Four-jaw chuck

In my opinion, the four-jaw chuck is one of the niftiest lathe accessories you can buy (*middle photo*). A four-jaw chuck (often referred to by one of many brand names, such as a Nova chuck, a Vicmarc chuck, or a Oneway Stronghold, Talon, or Scroll chuck) grips a workpiece with four jaws, which are tightened with a pair of metal rods or an Allen wrench. Because the jaws are beveled on the ends, they can be used to grip a similarly beveled recess in the bottom of a bowl, platter, or other object. Extremely versatile, these chucks typically cost around $200, and numerous accessory jaws are available.

DRILL CHUCKS

Another nifty chuck accessory for your lathe is a drill chuck (*bottom photo*). It's basically a drill chuck that fits onto one end of a Morse taper turning center. You can insert this chuck into the headstock to drive a round workpiece, or use it in the tailstock to hold a drill bit. This is the more common use for a drill chuck, as it excels at drilling a perfectly centered hole in a round workpiece—it's a great way to remove the bulk of the waste from a turned box. And if you use a true Forstner bit, you'll end up with a flat-bottomed hole.

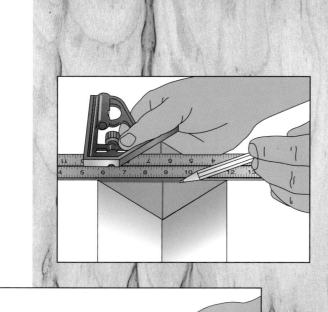

STOCK PREPARATION

Before you can mount a workpiece in the lathe, it must be prepared: Centerpoints need to be defined on the ends of spindles, and a kerf should be cut for the drive center.

Find the center

There are a number of ways you can quickly find the center of a workpiece. The combination square is the perfect tool for the job, with two different ways to use it to locate dead-center. The first and simplest method to locate center is to use the 45-degree head of the square to mark a series of diagonals (*top drawing*). This method works best with stock that is relatively square, since sides that are not 90-degree can throw the centerpoint off. If you've purchased the center-finding head for your combination square, it doesn't get any easier than this: Just slip the center-finding head on the blade and position the head so it touches adjacent sides of the workpiece; then mark center. This head is especially useful for finding center on round stock.

Kerfs for centers

The spurs on drive centers will stay sharper longer if you first make one or two diagonal kerfs in the end of the workpiece (*middle drawing*). This also makes it a lot easier to center the drive spur. Take a pass or two with a small gent's saw, and continue until the kerfs are about $^1/_8$" deep. Then drive the center in place.

CENTER FINDERS

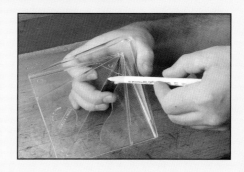

■ Finding the center of a workpiece is a common lay-out task. It's so common that a number of tool manufactur-ers make plastic center find-ers, like the one shown in the bottom photo, specifically for this task. These simple tools have lips on two adjacent sides to quickly position the workpiece so you can mark dead-center. To use a center finder, press the edges of the workpiece up against the lips of the center finder. Then butt a pencil or marking knife up against the center cutout and draw along this to mark a line on the workpiece. Next, rotate the workpiece 90 degrees and make another mark. Where the lines intersect is dead-center.

Drill clearance holes

In addition to saw kerfs, you may find it beneficial to drill clearance holes into the ends of the workpiece where the lines or kerfs intersect (*top photo*). This also helps the drive center "self-align" as it's driven into the end. It also makes it easier to align the opposite end in the tailstock. A $1/8$"- or $3/16$"-diameter bit works great—just drill about $1/4$" deep. Clearance holes like this are particularly useful when you're working with hardwoods, especially dense species like cocobolo or rosewood.

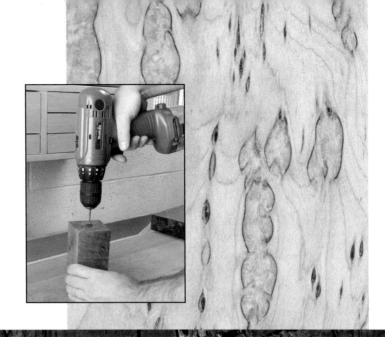

PREPARING STOCK FOR FACEPLATES

Faceplates are another type of chuck that allow you to turn plates, platters, bowls, and trays. Instead of gripping the wood like a four-jaw chuck, the workpiece is screwed to the face of the plate via holes in the plate. To prepare a blank for faceplate work, start by cutting the blank round and then attach the plate.

To make the workpiece round, first find the center and then use a compass to draw the circle size you want. I like to set my compass with a steel rule. I set the steel point into the etched graduation at the 1" mark and then adjust the drawing point to the desired radius (plus 1"). Although the steel point of a compass generally does an adequate job of holding its place, I've found that making a slight starter hole with an awl helps keep the point from wandering as the compass is rotated to mark the circle or arc (*middle photo*). Then cut out the shape with a band saw, saber saw, or scroll saw.

Before attaching the faceplate, it's best to drill shank holes in the workpiece for the screws. Here again, dense woods will benefit the most from this since screws driven in without shank holes tend to snap off. Make sure to use screws that are as large as will fit through the holes in the faceplate, and use as many as you can (*bottom photo*). The last thing you want is a workpiece flying off in your face.

USING A GOUGE

The catch phrase you'll hear over and over again from turning instructors is "make sure the bevel is rubbing." That's the secret to using most cutting tools. What it means is you should position the tool so it's supported by the tool rest and the bevel of the tool is riding on the workpiece. The simplest way to do this is to start with the handle pointing down. Place the bevel against the workpiece and raise the handle until cutting begins. As long as you keep the shank or blade of the tool against the tool rest and bevel on the workpiece, cutting should be smooth and sweet.

Tool rest position

There's some debate on tool rest placement. The placement that works best for you depends on the lathe height, your height, and your working stance. To find your tool rest position, start with the tool rest centered on the workpiece, and spin it by hand to make sure it clears the workpiece. You want to be as close to the workpiece as possible without making contact. Now make a test cut, turn off the lathe, and shift the rest up or down as needed. I prefer a tool rest that's slightly below center (*top photo*).

Roughing out

If the stock you've chucked in the lathe is square, select a low speed and present the tool (usually a roughing gouge) to the workpiece gently, but with a firm grip. I tend to skew the gouge at a slight angle as I move it along the tool rest (*middle photo*). Once the corners are knocked off, stop the lathe and move the tool rest closer to the workpiece. Continue like this until you've turned a cylinder.

QUICK CHECK FOR ROUNDNESS

Here's a lathe trick that's been around almost as long as lathes. It was developed by production turners who didn't want to shut off their lathes just to check whether their workpieces were round. What they did instead was leave the lathe on and place their turning tool gently on top of the spinning workpiece (*bottom photo*). If the workpiece was round, the tool was still. If it wasn't, the tool bounced up and down—the higher it bounced, the more work they had left. There's also a telltale "clicking" noise every time the tool encounters a flat surface. I have a blind woodworker friend that uses this to "listen" to see whether a workpiece is round or not.

CUTTING COVES

Coves are a nice decorative detail that can add visual interest to any spindle. They're surprisingly easy to turn, and with a little practice, you'll be making coves by the dozen.

Lay out coves

The first step in turning a cove is to lay out its exact position and width. Even if you're practicing, this is a good idea, because most coves you turn will be part of a pattern such as a spindle leg. Turn off the lathe, and locate the start and stop points of the cove. I generally make a full-sized template from $1/4$" hardboard to make duplicating parts easier—this also is a quick way to pick up diameters with a set of calipers. Just open them to fit over the template, and they're set. Turn on the lathe and you'll see a ghosted line from the marks you made. If you like, darken these lines by touching the tip of a pencil at the ghosted line (*top photo*).

Start the cove

I'll admit that the first coves I ever turned came out lousy. I thought all you had to do was shove a fingertip gouge into the wood and it'd cut a perfect cove. Well, it will cut a cove, but it'll tear the heck out of the edges. The proper way to turn a cove is to start with the gouge held almost vertical (*middle photo*). Then present the tool to the workpiece, and press in and roll the gouge so it ends up near horizontal—it's really a quick twist of the wrist—and one half of the cove is done.

Finish the cove

To finish the cove, start as you did for the first half, except on the other side. Here again, press in and twist to make the cut. With a little practice you can make a cove with two opposing cuts. If the two halves don't meet, pare away additional stock from the heavy side, using the same technique (*bottom photo*).

CUTTING BEADS

Beads are another decorative accent that are common on many turnings. Although not quite as simple as coves, they're fun to make.

Prepare the bead

To turn a bead, start by laying out its width and position. Use the same techniques that you used for coves. Next, because a bead sits proud of the spindle surface, you'll need to remove stock on both sides of the bead to provide clearance for your turning tools (*top photo*). In most cases, you'll be turning the spindle to its appropriate diameter anyway with either a spindle gouge or a skew chisel.

Start the bead

A bead is turned almost the opposite of a cove. Start with the gouge held vertically at the center of the bead. Then press in and twist your wrist to peel off shavings (*middle photo*). Slow down as you approach the spindle surface. Here again, with practice, one half of a small bead can usually be turned in a single pass (depending on its radius). Large coves will require several passes to remove the larger amount of stock, but the technique is the same.

Finish the bead

Just as with a cove, it's best to turn a bead as two halves. Reverse the gouge position so it starts at the center of the bead, and this time turn the opposite direction to remove the remaining shoulder (*bottom photo*). If the two halves don't match, trim the offending side with light paring cuts, using the same technique as you did to make the bead.

HOLLOWING WORK

Much of turning involves hollowing or removing waste with a gouge. Entire books have been written on bowl turning, and there's not sufficient space here for me to cover this challenging but rewarding pastime. I will, however, touch briefly on basic technique and share some tips I've picked up over the years.

Lay out hollow

Regardless of whether you're turning a plate, platter, bowl, or tray, you'll want to start by turning the bottom first. The reason for this is that the recess that you hollow out in the bottom can then be used by a 4-jaw chuck to grip the workpiece so you can turn the inside. This creates a finished product with no screw holes in the bottom (as you would if you used a faceplate). It also gives the piece a more finished look as well as helping the piece sit flat (a recessed bottom will handle surface irregularities better than a flat bottom). Start by marking the perimeter of the hollow on the workpiece with a pencil (*top photo*).

Begin hollowing

I do most of my hollowing work with a $1/2$" or $3/8$" fingertip gouge. Although you might think to just jab the gouge into the workpiece straight on, you'll find that you'll get a cleaner cut by presenting the tool to the workpiece at a slight angle (*middle photo*). This is known as a shear cut and creates a much cleaner cut—just as if you skewed a hand plane while planing. Since the cutting action takes place more on the side of the cutting tip instead of the end, this technique does require some practice. But keep at it—you'll be rewarded with flowing shavings and glass-smooth surfaces.

Finish the cut

There are two basic ways to make a hollowing cut: You can either start at the perimeter and work your way toward the center, or start at the center and work your way out toward the perimeter. I've always had best luck starting at the perimeter and working in (*bottom photo*), but try both ways to see which works best for you. If you're after an absolutely flat bottom, consider switching to a sharp square-edged scraper to make the final cuts.

USING A
SKEW CHISEL

As I mentioned earlier, the skew chisel is notorious for catching and digging into a workpiece. Besides proper technique, there are a couple other things you can do to tame this wild beast. First, I recommend filing a slight round-over on the bottom edges of the tool along its length. This helps the tool slide more easily along the tool rest so it can't catch or bump on it, which can cause the tip to catch the workpiece. Second, consider regrinding the profile of your chisel to form a gentle curve along the edge. Leave the top edge straight, and curve just the bottom—in effect, you're removing the sharp corner that's most likely to catch.

A light grip

One of the most difficult things to learn about using a skew chisel is to use a light grip. A death grip on this tool will only make your movements jerky, resulting in catches. Present the tool to the workpiece at an angle so neither the top nor bottom corner of the tip is contacting the workpiece (*top photo*). This limits the actual cutting area to about one-half to one-third of its edge—that's why the wider the chisel, the easier it is to use. I always recommend that beginners practice with the widest chisel they have on hand.

Watch those corners

Move the chisel slowly along the tool rest, with your attention focused on the corners of the tool (*middle photo*). You'll find that once you start a cut with the bevel rubbing on the workpiece, the chisel will almost feed itself into the workpiece as it moves along. Take the time to sharpen a skew chisel as you would a plane blade. Then take light cuts and use little pressure—let the tool do the work.

Shear cut

Although most folks use a skew chisel only for smoothing cylinders and gentle curves, it's also useful for fine detail work such as cutting clean V-grooves and chamfers. When used with its point down (*bottom drawing*), it makes a cleaner shoulder than a parting tool would (*see page* 189) because it cuts instead of scrapes.

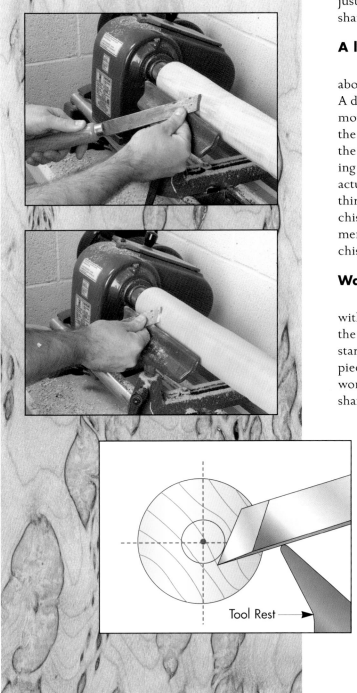

Tool Rest

USING A SCRAPER

Scrapers, if used properly, can leave a finish that rivals that of a sharp gouge or skew chisel. For a scraper to leave a finish this smooth, it must be prepared like a hand scraper. The business end must be ground and then honed smooth so that a fine burr can be rolled on the end. Granted, you can scrape without a burr, but you'll tear out the wood fibers, leaving a rough surface, instead of shearing them off.

Tilt the scraper down

Scrapers are extremely easy to use, and the only rule you need to follow religiously is to angle the end of the scraper down toward the lathe bed (*top drawing*). If you angle it up, a nasty catch can result. As always, keep the tool rest as close to the workpiece as possible while still allowing room for the lathe tool. When scraping a spindle, you'll generally want to raise the tool rest higher than you normally would so that when you tilt the scraper down, it contacts the workpiece near its center (*middle photo*).

Slicing versus scraping

The controversy over scraping versus cutting or slicing is one that will continue as long as there's more than two turners in the world. It really is a matter of personal preference, and in my mind there is no right or wrong answer. Much of the controversy is the result of improper scraping technique and poorly prepared scrapers. It's true that a cutting tool such as a skew chisel or gouge will produce a much smoother surface than one made with a poorly used or prepared scraper (*left and right halves of the cylinder, respectively, in the bottom photo*). But you can get the same result with a sharp scraper taking light cuts.

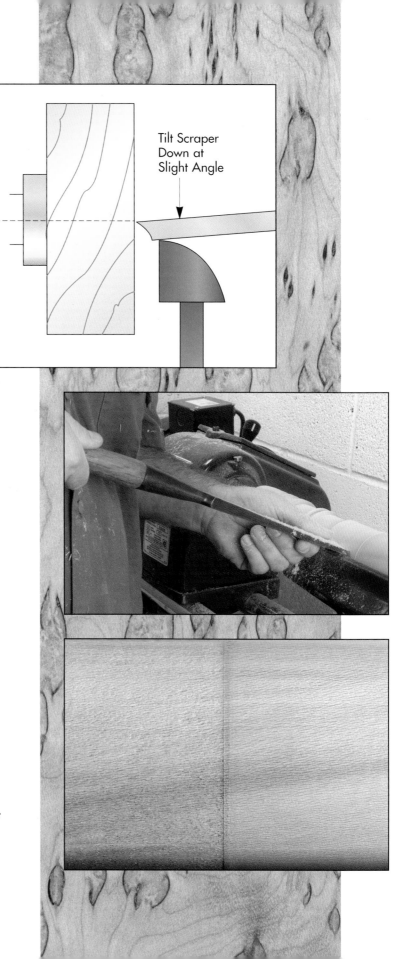

Tilt Scraper Down at Slight Angle

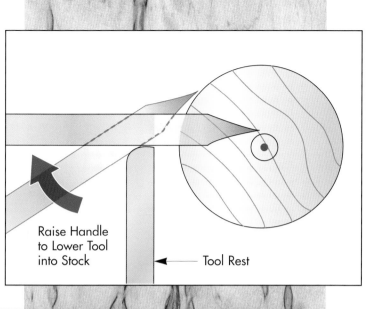

Raise Handle
to Lower Tool
into Stock

Tool Rest

PARTING OFF

A parting tool is actually a special scraper that's designed to prepare a spindle for removal from the lathe or to actually remove a part, or "part off" a portion, of a workpiece held in a chuck (such as removing the top of a turned box held in a four-jaw or screw chuck.

Tool position

The same tool and tool rest positions and technique that you used for scrapers are similar to those used with a parting tool. The only thing that's different is that you can present the tool to the workpiece so that it's centered on it and then begin the cut (*top drawing*). Then press down as you tilt the handle up (*middle photo*) to begin scraping. This will cut a kerf the same width as the parting tool in the workpiece.

Widen the kerf for clearance

If I've got sufficient stock left on the workpiece, I always widen the kerf that the parting tool makes by taking a series of light cuts (about $1/4$" to $1/2$" deep), alternating back and forth to create a double-wide kerf. I've found that this extra clearance prevents the tip of the parting tool from heating up because of the friction (*bottom photo*). With a single kerf, the sides of the tool tip are constantly rubbing against the workpiece. If you take a single, deep cut, it's quite possible to heat the tip to the point that you'll remove the temper from the steel.

A word of caution here: Make sure to wear gloves to "catch" a part that you're parting off, to protect yourself from splinters. Also, if you're preparing a spindle for removal, take care to leave sufficient stock so that the workpiece is still rigid. I've seen novice turners reduce the spindle diameter so far that the workpiece started to flex, then chatter, then fly off the lathe. This just isn't necessary, as you'll most likely cut the waste off with a saw anyway. What's one or two more saw strokes, compared to the possibility of a flying spindle?

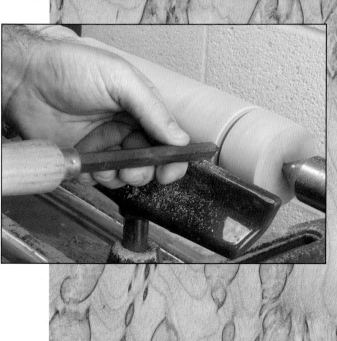

INDEX

METRIC EQUIVALENCY CHART

Inches to millimeters and centimeters

inches	mm	cm	inches	cm	inches	cm
1/8	3	0.3	9	22.9	30	76.2
1/4	6	0.6	10	25.4	31	78.7
3/8	10	1.0	11	27.9	32	81.3
1/2	13	1.3	12	30.5	33	83.8
5/8	16	1.6	13	33.0	34	86.4
3/4	19	1.9	14	35.6	35	88.9
7/8	22	2.2	15	38.1	36	91.4
1	25	2.5	16	40.6	37	94.0
1 1/4	32	3.2	17	43.2	38	96.5
1 1/2	38	3.8	18	45.7	39	99.1
1 3/4	44	4.4	19	48.3	40	101.6
2	51	5.1	20	50.8	41	104.1
2 1/2	64	6.4	21	53.3	42	106.7
3	76	7.6	22	55.9	43	109.2
3 1/2	89	8.9	23	58.4	44	111.8
4	102	10.2	24	61.0	45	114.3
4 1/2	114	11.4	25	63.5	46	116.8
5	127	12.7	26	66.0	47	119.4
6	152	15.2	27	68.6	48	121.9
7	178	17.8	28	71.1	49	124.5
8	203	20.3	29	73.7	50	127.0

mm = millimeters   cm = centimeters